GIVING VOICE TO
PROFOUND DISABILITY

THE UNIVERSITY OF
WINCHESTER

Giving _____ ith
profou _____ the
voices _____ th,
suppo _____ ing
parent _____ ers
philos _____ led
people _____

- R
- D
- F
- R
- V
- C

The e _____ ind
achiev _____ but
they a _____ lop
their f _____ to
this g _____ ace
equiv _____

Gi _____ the
lives c _____ ers,
nurses, therapists, academics, _____ ~~dents and policymakers.

John Vorhaus is _____ of London, UK.

GIVING VOICE TO PROFOUND DISABILITY

Dignity, dependence and human capabilities

John Vorhaus

Routledge
Taylor & Francis Group

LONDON AND NEW YORK

First published 2016
by Routledge
2 Park Square, Milton Park, Abingdon, Oxon OX14 4RN

and by Routledge
711 Third Avenue, New York, NY 10017

Routledge is an imprint of the Taylor & Francis Group, an informa business

© 2016 J. Vorhaus

British Library Cataloguing in Publication Data
A catalogue record for this book is available from the British Library

Library of Congress Cataloging in Publication Data
Vorhaus, John (Philosopher)
Giving voice to profound disability : dignity, dependence and human capabilities / John Vorhaus.
pages cm
1. People with disabilities--Care. 2. People with disabilities--Education. I. Title.
HV1568.V67 2015
362.4'04--dc23
2015001044

ISBN: 978-0-415-73162-1 (hbk)
ISBN: 978-0-415-73163-8 (pbk)
ISBN: 978-1-315-69371-2 (ebk)

Typeset in Bembo
by Saxon Graphics Ltd, Derby

Printed and bound by Ashford Colour Press Ltd., Gosport Hampshire

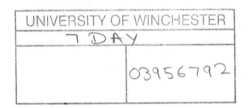

MIX
Paper from
responsible sources
FSC
www.fsc.org   FSC® C011748

Dedicated to Vi Boorman and Janet Melrose

CONTENTS

ACKNOWLEDGEMENTS

I first began to learn about disability and profound dependency, and to appreciate the priceless value of good care, when my father developed Motor Neurone Disease and (his wife having passed away) he was looked after by two women in his local community, Vi Boorman and Janet Melrose. Between them they displayed many of the virtues I have since witnessed or learned of in the context of caring for people with profound disabilities. My father never lost his dignity, and, despite progressive and eventual total paralysis, the last three years were among the richest of his life. That is a testament to devoted and skilled attentiveness, and it was the shining example of Vi and Janet that first set me on the way to thinking about profound disability, dependency and care; hence the book's dedication.

In accordance with ethical guidelines, the names of almost every person and organisation contributing to this book have been anonymised. This is as it should be; but it has the frustrating consequence that I am not able to name each of the 102 people, including teachers and parents from five schools, who generously gave their time, and some of whose words and experience make up the bulk of this book. From them I learned more than I can say, and certainly more than I have managed to write about. If I have succeeded in conveying even a small fraction of the insight and understanding shared by my interviewees, then this exercise will have been worthwhile.

Academics often need all the support they can get, and I would like to thank Charlie Farrar, Chrissie Rogers and Eva Kittay for providing moral support at a formative stage in the process of putting my thoughts together.

Writing is a solitary, often anti-social activity; when writing one is not, for example, giving time to family. For uncomplaining acceptance of this drawn out intrusion, and for gracious moral support at home, I give grateful thanks to my wife, Jennifer, and our children, Elise and Liesel.

The important thing is what this book documents: the value and achievements of people whose disabilities render them incapable of talking about the subjects discussed here; and the lives of people given over to others – their labour and sacrifice, and the good things that they do. This book is designed to acknowledge and give some voice to their lives and works.

Permissions

Earlier versions of fragments of Chapters 2, 3, 4, 5 and 7 have appeared previously in: 'Philosophy and profound disability: learning from experience', *Disability and Society*, 2014, 29, 4: 611–623 (Chapters 2 and 4); 'Capabilities, human value and profound disability', *Disability and Society*, forthcoming 2015 (Chapters 2, 3 and 5); 'Capability, freedom and profound disability', *Disability and Society*, 2013, 28, 8: 1047–1058 (Chapter 3); and 'Respecting Profoundly Disabled Learners', in *Journal of Philosophy of Education*, 2006, 40, 3: 313–328 (Chapter 7). I am grateful to editors and publishers for kind permission to reprint revised versions of previously published material.

1

INTRODUCTION

This is a book about people with profound and multiple learning difficulties and disabilities (PMLD) – people who, in the main, cannot write or speak much for themselves – and those who are best able to speak up on their behalf – their parents, carers and teachers. Books on disability would fill many libraries; books on profound and multiple disabilities a few shelves; and books devoted to exploring the lives of profoundly disabled people, and the experience of those who care for and work with them, rather less than that. It is the last of these that this book is given over to.

It is not so long ago that any such exercise would have been regarded as eccentric. Times are changing: in recent years we have witnessed the growth of disability rights movements, the emergence of disability studies as a multi-disciplinary activity in its own right, and such legislative landmarks as the 1995 UK Disability Discrimination Act (DDA), as amended by the Special Educational Needs and Disability Act 2001, and the Americans with Disabilities Act Amendments Act 2008. Notable recent policy initiatives in England include Healthcare for All (2008), an inquiry into access to healthcare for people with learning disabilities, and the Children and Families Act (2014), which includes legislation to support children and families with special educational needs. A significant review, more closely focused on the people discussed here, is the Salt Review (2010) into the supply of teachers for pupils with severe, profound and multiple learning difficulties. I will be returning to this review in due course.

In writing this book, I had two principal aims: to provide some insight into the lives of people with profound learning difficulties and disabilities, and of those who are closest to them, and to offer introductory thoughts on some of the broad philosophical issues that arise from reflection on profound disability. I say 'philosophical' issues, and they are that, but they also number among the basic questions and conundrums that any person who lives and works with profound disability will come up against at one time or another: questions about love and care, dignity and respect, dependence and independence, human capabilities and the value of human beings.

I am not aware of other work having aims that precisely match these; but I have learned much from writers who have sought to include the experiences of people with profound and other cognitive disabilities in their own theoretical research on disability (*Disability and Society* 1999; Knox et al. 2000; Chappell 2000; Brett 2002).

Giving voice to profound disability

It is easy to state these aims, more difficult to do justice to them. Though I have sought to 'give voice to profound disability', it has not been possible to include the voices of profoundly disabled people themselves. It is certainly possible to communicate with people with profound disabilities, and to elicit their thoughts on many matters that affect them, including their needs, wants and preferences. It is a challenge of a different order, however, when what is wanted is reflection on one's status, value and capabilities. There is a pressing question, one which developments in technology and pedagogy should assist with, as to what more can be done to utilise and develop forms of augmentative and alternative communication,[1] so as to enable profoundly disabled people to communicate, and, among other things, to contribute to a research exercise of this kind. The absence of testimony from profoundly disabled people is, it must be said, a conspicuous omission; nevertheless, I have sought to give ample space to those who are closest to people with PMLD, and, as far as possible, I have allowed the people I interviewed to speak for themselves, both when describing their own experience and when offering thoughts on the questions this book is designed to look into.

This is not a work of social science. It would even be misleading to say that the experiences presented here are drawn from a 'sample' of carers and professionals, since the group of people I interviewed was not identified in accordance with sampling methodology. The process of finding respondents was largely opportunistic; most interviewees live and work in south-east England, which is also where the five schools I have spent time in are located. The testimony is collected from interviews undertaken over five years with 102 people who parent, live with, care for, teach or otherwise work closely with people with profound disabilities: parents, grandparents, (extended) family members, support workers, head teachers, teachers, learning support assistants and interpreters, along with miscellaneous others, including neurologists, musicologists, theatre directors and religious leaders. Particularly with respect to carers and teachers, I sought out voices representing numerous ethnicities, and people of varying ages and socio-economic backgrounds. Most interviewees are women, in keeping with the profile of primary carers and teachers of people with profound disabilities. And most of the profoundly disabled people discussed here are either children or young people, aged between 3 and 25 years.[2] The interviews tended to last between 1 and 2 hours: they had a common structure but they also allowed respondents to explore any of those aspects of living with profound disability that were of greatest interest or were otherwise pre-occupying.

I encouraged respondents to speak at length, and candidly, about their experience. But, owing to personality, or culture, or both, not everyone is able or willing to disclose their innermost thoughts, some of which may be painful or embarrassing, or relate to something which it would be easier not to face head on. In any case, it is a big 'ask' to invite someone to talk openly about their love for or their life with a person with profound disabilities. Profound disabilities present daunting challenges: some people were understandably reluctant to disclose what they might consider as intimate details of their private lives, or to discuss some of the feelings that go along with a demanding relationship – anger, for example, or envy of others' good fortune. One respondent, Cheryl Arvidson-Keating, an eloquent and outspoken mother of a profoundly disabled girl, is well aware of the sensitivities and complications. Shortly after our interview she posted the following thoughts on a blog:

> My experience … is that there is an Inner and an Outer world. The 'Inner World' [includes] people who understand how you are living … people with similar lives that you meet at the hospice or the disabled parent support group; in the Consultant's waiting room or at the Wheelchair Skills Training Course … You may also have a few close friends that are also in your 'inner world', who you can vent to, who *get it*. Your child's professionals may or may not get it, it depends on their experience, their empathy and how closely you work with them.
>
> And then, there is everyone else. They are in the 'Outer World'. They are the people who you keep a smile in your pocket for. When they ask how you are doing, you don't tell them that you were awake four times turning N in the night and then spent twenty minutes scrubbing feed off the carpet and had to bath and change her before you went out because she tried to help you hold the bolus and her co-ordination was so poor this morning that it went everywhere, so you were late taking L to school again and she was unsettled and didn't want to go and you were late getting back to pick N up to take her to her short-notice Orthotics appointment you got because her splints are so painful that she can't walk in them – and therefore at all – and so you didn't have time to park at the hospital and you fumbled getting N from the car seat to the wheelchair and ricked your back and she was grumpy and wouldn't let the Orthoticist look at her feet without you holding her whilst she screamed and … so on.
>
> You just get the smile out, paste it on and say '*Oh, we're fine! How about you?*' Because you know that if you do start talking, you'll start crying with exhaustion; and they aren't close enough to you to have to deal with that.
>
> I have to trust you a very great deal to let you in to my inner world in real life. So I say, to you 'Outer World' people … parent-carers of disabled children do talk about … grief … anger and desperation. We just don't talk

about it with you. And it's not because we are deliberately excluding you –
at least, that's not my reason. It's just that it's such a huge thing to explain
that it's simpler to paste on the smile and talk about other stuff.

(*Arvidson-Keating 2014*)

Some parent-carers will experience less grief and anger than others; but anyone
should be able to understand the principal point that Cheryl is expressing. I, being
neither close friend nor confidant, represent the 'Outer World', with all that that
implies for the ability and preparedness of respondents to open up to me.

Regardless of candour or inhibition, it should be no surprise if parental
reflections turn out to be partial, or sanguine, or based more on hope than
expectation. The perspective of a neuro-disability specialist is helpful here. Michelle
is a consultant paediatric neurologist who has worked with profoundly disabled
children and their families for many years. She is the first to admit that in the
process of arriving at judgements about treatment, including life-saving treatment,
the knowledge and experience of patients and their families is indispensable; as it is
for making judgements about someone's existing and anticipated quality of life, a
judgement that will feature in any decision about whether to resuscitate a child, or
to keep her alive. Michelle remarks that 'intensivists' – specialists providing care
and treatment to patients in intensive care – may only gain first-hand knowledge
of patients and their families in that one context. They cannot see for themselves
how patients and families adjust to their lives and constraints over time. The
intensivist may see grief and despair when the diagnosis is first disclosed, but not
how strong and resilient people can be; how, one year later, two years later, the
child who was struggling to live, and the parents who were struggling to keep
themselves from falling apart, may all have adapted to the point that they are now
well, and coping well, with their new lives.

On the other hand, Michelle can see that parents are not always the best judges
of their children's prospects, or what their children are likely to be capable of. It is
always her intention to learn as much from the parents and children as time allows,
and she is the first to acknowledge that parents are often a good judge of their
child's capabilities; but there are also examples of parents with inflated expectations
of their child, or whose beliefs and expectations are at odds with testimony from
other sources – reports from schools and physiotherapists for example. If a parent
is saying one thing, whilst all the evidence is suggesting another, there is inevitably
a question about the extent to which the parent has hold of the whole truth.

Of course it is the most natural thing in the world for a parent to hope against
hope, or to believe that her child will walk unaided or communicate with words
when all the evidence suggests that this will not be possible. And sometimes, against
(almost) all expectation, a parent turns out to have been closer to the truth about
her children than anyone else. At the very least, hopes and aspirations should be
treated with care, even if they are destined to be disappointed. Whilst, therefore, it
is necessary to consider whether a feeling or a hope has a basis in fact, it is also
important to show sensitivity to what carers believe and yearn for, even if the facts

remain obstinately set against them. In any case, it is sometimes hard to ascertain what the 'facts' are, or where the line between 'fact' and 'aspiration' lies exactly; moreover, believing that something is so, and willing it to be so – 'my daughter *will* learn to walk, no matter what it takes!' – can make it more likely that it *becomes* so one day. The pursuit of dreams and sheer determination can make a difference to how things turn out – to what is, after all, possible. This is taking us into the realm of philosophy.

Philosophical reflections

The second of the book's aims is to provide some philosophical reflection on the experiences described here. It is closely related to the first, since I intend to illustrate the importance of human testimony for philosophical thinking about disability, as provided by those closest to people with profound disabilities. Their experience has weight, both because it is their experience and because of the illumination it casts on some of the more abstract questions that philosophy deals with.

The discussions to follow are intended as an introduction to a few of the many philosophical questions raised by reflection on profound disability – about dignity, respect, care, dependency, human capabilities and the value of human beings. My intention is to introduce these subjects (no more than that), to show how they are related to each other, and how each is pertinent not only to the lives of profoundly disabled people but also to all of us at some stages in our lives. There are numerous other questions barely mentioned here – about personhood, identity, power, oppression, freedom and justice – which I could equally well have chosen to concentrate on, and about which philosophers of disability have written extensively (Kittay 1999; Francis and Silvers 2000; Carlson 2010).

The philosophical questions that *are* discussed go to the heart of what many of us value and care about. But it is not always easy to articulate and explain basic values, nor what they imply for how we should behave. Consider how we think about respecting people and their dignity: that we should show respect for people and not violate their human dignity are among our most basic precepts, and they are included in regulations specifying standards of conduct in educational and other institutional settings. However, whilst there is a consensus that these precepts should inform the ethos and pedagogy found in special schools, it is much less clear what their practical and theoretical implications are or should be. Ought we always to judge, to take a practical example, that we are failing to show respect for a pupil if we choose to talk over her head, if she cannot understand what we are saying, or even appreciate *that* we are indeed talking over her head? Or, to take a theoretical example, does respect for persons imply that a principal pedagogic goal is the promotion of pupil's autonomy, even as this applies to a child with a life-limiting condition who is in a lot of pain, and for whom any new routine will induce considerable distress?

I will seek to show how the experiences described here illuminate philosophical questions such as these. To do that it is necessary to have an eye to the philosopher's perennial concerns with truth and argument; to claim no more on behalf of someone's testimony than their testimony warrants; to notice any inconsistencies; and to be aware of any evidence that might either support or detract from the truth or plausibility of what has been said.

A great deal has been written about 'truth' and 'interpretation' in the context of disability, but I shall not offer much discussion here.[3] I aim to show respect for truth and consistency, but I also seek to allow ample room for people's interpretations of experience; and not only their interpretations, but also their hopes and aspirations, for these too play a sustaining role in the lives of those who care for and teach profoundly disabled people.

The question, 'Is it true that this child is and always will be profoundly disabled?' misleadingly suggests a simple answer. It might be true that she is profoundly disabled, owing to a genetic endowment, or it might be true not only in virtue of that, but also in virtue of how she is perceived by significant others and in the eyes of society generally. The 'social model' of disability draws attention to the extent to which disability is related to perceptions, attitudes and assumptions embedded in the culture of a society. On this model the term 'disability' is reserved for incapacity whose source lies in societal practices, whilst 'impairment' is the term preferred for incapacities whose genesis has a neurological and genetic explanation. This terminological development is just one of many advances made by writers working on theoretical models of disability. Since this is not in the main a theoretical book, there is not space to discuss the social model of disability here, although it is hoped that the writing shows sensitivity to its many insights.

Throughout, the philosophical discussion is designed to supplement and grow out of reflections provided by the people I spoke with. Indeed, the relationship between their testimony and any philosophical discussion is reciprocal: the experiences described here inform philosophical reflections, just as these reflections are intended to illuminate, or sanction, or raise a question about some of the more prevalent beliefs, claims and ideas expressed by interviewees.

'Profound and multiple learning difficulties and disabilities'

Although mindful of recommendations under the social model, I have made extensive use of the term 'disability' in this book, including in the phrase 'profound and multiple learning difficulties and disabilities'. This phrase has kept its place since it is used and preferred by almost all the people I have spoken to, and it remains in common parlance in special schools in England, and in policy literature on disability. This may prove temporary, since the terms 'impairment' and 'disability' mark a real and important distinction. Nevertheless, I would ask readers who prefer alternative phrases to allow this concession to domestic nomenclature. At the very least, I aim, throughout, not to make any unwarranted assumptions about the scope, nature or source of any disability referred to.

This explains why the phrase 'profound and multiple learning difficulties and disabilities' is retained; but I should say more about how it tends to be used and understood, and how as a category it is distinguished from other categories of disability. Conceptions of PMLD remain a source of controversy: there is some dispute about the terms, categories and methods of measurement used to identify the forms and degrees of profound impairment, and the various dimensions to be taken account of – behavioural, physiological, emotional, and so on (Ouvry 1987: 12–16; Cleland 1979: 1–4). There is, moreover, an ongoing debate about the implied distinction between 'severe' and 'profound' disability, and what any definition of PMLD implies for levels of support and autonomy (Tassé et al. 2013). In the past the World Health Organisation (WHO) had suggested several categories of what it then referred to as 'retardation', relating each category to an IQ range. The categories included mild mental retardation (IQ 50–69), moderate mental retardation (IQ 35–49), severe mental retardation (IQ 20–34) and profound mental retardation. This last was characterised thus:

> The IQ is under 20. Comprehension and use of language is limited to, at best, understanding basic commands and making simple requests. The most basic and simple visuo-spatial skills of sorting and matching may be acquired, and the affected person may be able with appropriate supervision and guidance to take a small part in domestic and practical tasks. An organic aetiology can be identified in most cases. Severe neurological or other physical disabilities affecting mobility are common, as are epilepsy and visual and hearing impairments. Pervasive developmental disorders in their most severe form, especially atypical autism, are particularly frequent, especially in those who are mobile.
>
> *(WHO 1992: 230)*

Questions remain about the validity and reliability of the standard instruments used to measure intelligent quotients at any IQ levels, and especially at the lowest levels. In recent advice to WHO, the American Association on Intellectual and Developmental Disabilities (AAIDD) recommended that 'profound' and 'severe' learning disabilities are treated as a single category on the grounds that 'collapsing all individuals with IQ scores below 40 into one category is more scientifically and psychometrically supported' than attempting to impose a classificatory cut-off point five standard deviations below the population mean (i.e., IQ 5–25). In short: 'existing standardized tests of intelligence cannot reliably or validly distinguish individuals with IQ scores below 40' (Tassé et al. 2013: 127, 129).

The Diagnostic and Statistical Manual of Mental Disorder (DSM-IV-TR) describes profound disability as including 'considerable impairment in sensorimotor functioning', 'retardation with some neurological condition' and as requiring the 'constant need for 'pervasive support' (DSM-IV-TR 2000: 43–44). In the fifth edition of the DSM, profound disability in the social domain is such that 'the individual has very limited understanding of symbolic communication … express[ing] … desires and emotions largely through nonverbal, non-symbolic communication'. And in the practical domain the 'individual is dependent on others for all aspects of daily physical care, health and safety' (DSM-V 2013: 58, 61).

Each of these past and present stipulations has been variously interpreted, and it will emerge that the category of PMLD does not always lend itself to simple generalisations about its boundaries and what should be included within them. Moreover, many of the permissible generalisations are provisional, since much remains to be discovered about the capacities of people with profound disabilities. The tendency in the past was to underestimate potential, partly because educational and other developmental interventions were either not thought of or badly conceived, and partly because social expectations were set as low as they were. There is no reason to think that this tendency has been eliminated.

In the most general terms it is widely agreed that, in addition to extensive learning and cognitive disabilities, people with PMLD will have a combination of physical disabilities, sensory impairments and developmental disorders. In their review of literature, Dee et al. suggest that profoundly disabled people share two characteristics: a profound cognitive impairment or learning difficulty and a complex aggregation of difficulties in more than one area of their lives (2002: 4). Likewise, Lacey asserts that people with profound and multiple learning disabilities face difficulties of two kinds: 'They have more than one disability and ... one of these is profound intellectual impairment' (1998: ix).

The Salt Review was commissioned by the United Kingdom government to examine the supply of teachers trained to meet the needs of pupils with severe or profound and multiple learning difficulties and disabilities. This is the definition of PMLD proposed in the review, and subsequently adopted by the Department for Education:

> Pupils with profound and multiple learning difficulties have complex learning needs. In addition to very severe learning difficulties, pupils have other significant difficulties, such as physical disabilities, sensory impairment or a severe medical condition. Pupils require a high level of adult support, both for their learning needs and also for their personal care. They are likely to need sensory stimulation and a curriculum broken down into very small steps. Some pupils communicate by gesture, eye pointing or symbols, others by very simple language. Their attainments are likely to remain in the early P scale range (P1–P4) throughout their school careers (that is below level 1 of the National Curriculum).[4]
>
> *(Salt 2010: 14)*

A footnote adds: 'It is important to be clear that PMLD does *not* include pupils who have complex medical needs without any associated cognitive difficulties' (ibid.).

I adopt an understanding of 'profound and multiple learning difficulties and disabilities' that is consistent with the definition offered by the Salt Review. But there are many distinctions and complexities that this phrase might encourage us to overlook, and which will often be the subject of discussions to follow.

Profoundly disabled people in England

Whilst this book is not only about profoundly disabled people in England, but also about profound disability generally, it is worth providing a brief snapshot of the PMLD population in England, so as to give some idea of how many people are thought to have profound disabilities in a country of approximately 56 million people, and of how many schools cater for profoundly disabled children.

The Centre for Disability Research has provided estimates of existing and predicted numbers of adults and children with PMLD in England. The estimates are based on assumptions of varying degrees of reliability; in particular, there is uncertainty about predictions of estimated mortality rates, although the overall pattern of predictions remains consistent even if mortality rates vary substantially (Emerson 2009: ii).

The number of children aged under 18 with PMLD living in England in 2008 was estimated at 14,744; the number of adults aged 18 or over was estimated at 16,036 in 2008, and 16,234 in 2009. The figure for adults was projected to rise to 22,035 by 2026, with an average annual percentage increase of 1.8 per cent (ibid.: 5, 7). These figures suggest that, 'in an "average" area in England with a population of 250,000, the number of adults with people with PMLD receiving health and social care services will rise from 78 in 2009 to 105 in 2026, and that the number of young people with PMLD becoming adults in any given year will rise from 3 in 2009 to 5 in 2026' (ibid.: ii). These rates 'will be higher in communities that: (1) have a younger demographic profile; or (2) contain a greater proportion of citizens from Pakistani and Bangladeshi communities' (ibid.: 7). The estimates give evidence of a sustained and accelerating growth in the number of adults with PMLD in England, the acceleration owing to an increase in birth rates in the general population (ibid.: 7).

Consistent with Emerson's data, there is evidence of a rising number of *pupils* in England having PMLD (Male and Rayner 2007; Male 2009), and increased survival rates and more effective clinical interventions are likely to contribute to a further increase in the PMLD school population (Emerson and Hatton, 2008). The Salt Review suggested that in 2009 there were approximately 9,000 pupils with PMLD in the education system in the United Kingdom; 82 per cent of these were educated in special schools, 15 per cent in maintained primary schools and 3 per cent in maintained secondary schools. In their national survey of pupils with PMLD in England, Male and Rayner (2007) found that there were more boys with PMLD than girls (approximately 2:1) and that PMLD was more common among Pakistani and Bangladeshi children than among other ethnic groups. More than half of head teachers considered that their PMLD pupil population had increased 'significantly' or 'somewhat' in recent years, and that these pupils had increasingly complex needs (Male and Rayner 2007; Male 2009).

The profiles of national and school-based populations will vary from one country to the next, but it would be a surprise if the tendency observed here was not shared in many parts of the world – that of a population of people with PMLD that is not only growing, but also growing at an increasing rate from one year to the next.

The scope of this book

This book is, first and foremost, about people with profound and multiple learning difficulties and disabilities; hence the need to have some idea of who exactly we are talking about and the numbers of people to whom this description applies. If, indeed, profoundly disabled people were the exclusive object of attention, this would be more than justified, for reasons that should already be apparent, and also because they number among the most 'vulnerable members of our society today' (Michael 2008). But in fact, although profoundly disabled people constitute the primary focus, they are not the only people on whom the discussion has some bearing; for it is a significant objective to explore features of their lives that are common to all of us at one point or another – dependency, vulnerability, the need for care, and the need to be, and the need to be treated as being, a somebody and not a nobody. These are characteristics that apply not only to the 9,000 or so pupils with profound disabilities in England in 2008, or to the then English population of about 30,000 profoundly disabled people, but to every human being, irrespective of their abilities and disabilities.

Advice for readers

Any author would wish that their book is read from beginning to end, and I share that wish myself. But reading a book from cover to cover is a sizeable undertaking, particularly if it contains sections that are heavy going, as people who are not philosophers may find anything that is remotely philosophical. I suggest, therefore, for those for whom philosophy is anathema, or a little off-putting, that you skip the philosophical bits at first – particularly Chapters 3, 6 and 9 – and read only the stories and words of the interviewees, which, in any case, make up a good portion of the whole. There should be enough there for anyone to get their teeth into. But I suggest only that you skip the philosophy 'at first': the philosophical questions are not levered in from the outside, as it were; they emerge quite naturally from the thoughts and experiences of people whose voices make up the bulk of this book. And if some of the philosophy is hard, then – I feel bound to say – that is not my fault; the questions are intrinsically difficult, and there is no way of getting around that.

I have made every effort to use plain English, not quite always, but almost always. I make minimal use of footnotes and other technical devices that would be out of place here. And whilst I make occasional use of acronyms, I seek to keep these to a minimum.[5] As far as possible I avoid becoming embroiled in theoretical discussion of difficult concepts that crop up from time to time – concepts such as 'truth', as applied to what parents say and believe about their children, or 'human dignity', as applied to the status of profoundly disabled people – although I do need to say something about each of these. This, doubtless, will frustrate the more philosophically inclined, so I should say at the outset that this book is intended as offering only the most introductory discussion of the philosophical questions that feature here. The principal objective is simply to raise these questions and to illustrate their importance and complexity; nothing more. In any case, that is likely to suffice for most readers, and for anyone looking for more advanced philosophy that can be found in the texts included in the 'recommended reading' at the end of the book.

Synopsis

I will explore several dimensions of the lives of profoundly disabled people: their capabilities, dependency, value, dignity and care. I allow ample space for people both to talk about their experience and to reflect on it, and many sections of the book are taken up with their words, not mine. On three subjects – capabilities, valuing profoundly disabled people and caring for them – I judged it beneficial to include chapters on some of the theoretical questions that tend to be discussed, but readers are not obliged to agree, and those who do not may prefer to move swiftly on.

The capabilities of profoundly disabled people

Chapter 2 explores the great variety of capabilities among people with profound disabilities and the numerously inventive ways in which their capabilities are uncovered and developed. I look at the progress that people make in their lives, whether by small steps or large, and consider the lives of children for whom progress is inevitably limited and sometimes no longer possible. I examine how progress is assessed in the context of school curricula, and ask whether the contributions of profoundly disabled people – to their relationships, schools and communities – are always entirely captured by the language of 'capabilities'.

In an introduction to the theory on human capabilities, offered in Chapter 3, I explore how capability theory is expounded by Amartya Sen and Martha Nussbaum, two of its best-known advocates. The chapter is designed both to acknowledge the contribution of capability theory to our understanding of the condition of profoundly disabled people and to express some scepticism about the extent of that contribution. I suggest that capability theory exaggerates the importance of human agency and freedom in the context of what is of fundamental importance for any human being, and in particular, for people with profound disabilities.

Dependence and reciprocity

No matter what our range of capabilities, large or small, we are all dependent on others, particularly at the beginning and end of life, and not only then. Eva Kittay writes that dependency 'is not only an *exceptional* circumstance' and that to see it as such 'reflects an outlook that dismisses the importance of human interconnectedness' (1999: 29). It is one purpose of this book to illustrate the interconnectedness Kittay speaks of, including in the discussion of caring for and valuing other people. In Chapter 4 the emphasis is less on the carer and caring relations and more on dependent people themselves. I offer a series of pen portraits, and discuss dependencies and reciprocal relationships, along with the conflicting priorities that arise when the level of dependency leaves a doubt about the possibility of reciprocity and the value of pursuing independence.

Valuing profoundly disabled people

Chapters 5 and 6 look at the value and moral status of human beings with PMLD. In Chapter 5 we hear from parents who speak unreservedly about their love for their children, and explore how love reveals what is most precious in a human being. We learn of the difficulties that arise when love and care are not always returned or recognised, but also how much profoundly disabled children bring to people's lives, whether or not love is reciprocated in kind, and irrespective of any capacity for verbal communication. Faith and non-religious conviction lie at the centre of the lives of many parents and teachers, as is briefly discussed, whilst in the final section we see how easy it is to run out of words when discussing love and the value of a human life, not least because these can be such difficult subjects to find adequate words for.

No one who contributed to this book had any doubt that children and adults with PMLD are as important and precious as anyone else. And yet there are questions about our value that are not easy to answer. How should we explain the value of human beings, and how is this related to our moral status? Are human beings *equally* valuable, and, if so, what accounts for our equal value? The value of a human being can be thought about from several points of view: as it is revealed in our personal relationships, and in our dealings with those we love and care for; as expressed in the context of moral rights and duties that apply to all persons, whether or not we are personally related to them; and in the context of politics, including the rights and entitlements that attach to persons in virtue of their status as citizens. This last is discussed in Chapter 3, whilst in Chapter 6 I discuss how we value people from the personal and moral points of view.

Dignity and respect

Most of us believe that all human beings have dignity – human dignity – and that each of us should be treated with a basic respect. But what exactly is 'human dignity' and what do we mean when we say that everyone ought to be treated with respect?

These are not easy questions; nor is it always easy to know whether how we are speaking to, or holding or otherwise treating a profoundly disabled person is consistent with showing respect for their dignity. She may not be able to tell us; she may not even recognise our behaviour as being either consistent with her dignity or as amounting to a clear violation of it. In Chapter 7 I begin by looking at examples of how teachers and carers talk about treating someone with respect. I then explore what the basis of dignity and respect might be, including the idea that respect for a person essentially involves making an effort to see the world from their point of view, I look at the various ways in which we can see someone, either as a person, or as someone less than a person, and I explore why it matters that someone with PMLD should be seen as a person, including the importance of their being acknowledged by and connected to other people.

Caring for profoundly disabled people

The quality of the lives of people with profound and multiple learning difficulties depends in large measure on how well they are cared for. Chapter 8 includes accounts of what it is like to live with and care for a child who is profoundly dependent. The demands on carers differ one to another, and each day in the life of each carer is different. Even so, it is worth recording the experiences of a handful of carers, for although each of their stories is unique, each also includes many features that characterise the lives of most people who care for highly dependent children: the routines and arrangements, demands and impositions, anxieties and frustrations, the tiredness and 'never-endingness' of care – along with the surprises, satisfactions, rewards and joys.

Chapter 9 serves as an introduction to the theory of caring – what it is, why it matters and its role in an ethic of care. I explore the idea of caring, and how it has been variously conceived, and examine how caring is related to feelings, practices, knowledge and trust. I also take a look at the idea of caring relations, and, in particular, at how to give an account of reciprocity between carer and cared-for that does justice to the contribution of people with profound disabilities.

Looking ahead

The book ends by reflecting on a number of emerging themes and on the wealth of experience shared by the many contributors. I explore the potential for further enquiry, both in the way of collecting testimony, including from profoundly disabled people themselves, and in the way of collaborative research between practitioners and the academic community.

Recommended reading

For each of the principal subjects explored here, I recommend a handful of philosophical books that I have found to be especially valuable, and which offer discussions that are more advanced than anything presented in these pages.

Notes

1   That is, communication methods used to supplement or replace speech or writing for those with impairments in the production or comprehension of spoken or written language.
2   It would be a valuable exercise to conduct a study of this kind focused on older people.
3   These are difficult subjects, requiring a subtle treatment, and any discussion that is either perfunctory or inexpert is likely not to be worth embarking upon.
4   The P scales were created by the Qualifications and Curriculum Authority (QCA) in order to assess children who did not attain at least Level 1 on the National Curriculum.
5   This includes use of the acronym 'PMLD', which has its place, but which should not monopolise the means of identifying the group of people it refers to.

2

HUMAN CAPABILITIES

In practice

1 Introduction

It might seem as if the only safe thing to say about people with profound and multiple learning difficulties is that this is a group defined by having limited and underdeveloped capabilities, or by their simply lacking some of the basic capabilities altogether. Yet the capabilities of people with PMLD are typically greater and more various than one might expect. Many people will vocalise extensively although very few are able to use any language; many contribute as much to relationships as anyone might, whilst the interaction of others is more confined; some are keenly aware of themselves as separate persons, others have limited awareness of even their own bodies. And one and the same person may have emotional intelligence but no language, play the piano whilst being unable to brush her teeth, or use a computer and yet be at risk if left alone for even a moment. And there are many surprises: some children develop far in excess of anyone's expectations.

Not everyone, however, has high expectations. Elisabeth Peters, Head of Christ Church School for children with severe and profound learning difficulties and disabilities, recalls a visit from a teacher working in a Romanian special school. During a tour of Christ Church, the visitor became increasingly perplexed before asking, finally: 'Where are your children in cots? We have our profoundly disabled children in cots all day.' Elisabeth pointed to the children with PMLD, seated on the floor, playing with coloured card and sticky paper: 'There are your children in cots!' As she later remarked: 'If you do nothing, they will do nothing. Once you start the interaction, wake up their senses, they wake up, they emerge, and you see that they want to be active, to be stimulated, to engage with us.'

In this chapter, starting with section 2, I explore the variety of capabilities among people with profound disabilities and the numerously inventive ways in which their capabilities are uncovered and developed. In section 3 I look at how children develop and progress in their lives, and I consider children for whom progress is inevitably limited and sometimes no longer possible. And in section 4 I take a brief look at how progress and capabilities are assessed in the context of school curricula for children with PMLD.

2 Revealing capabilities

Theatre and humour

I begin with the world of theatre, and an example of an innovative approach to uncovering capabilities, one which shows great sensitivity to the senses and sensibilities of children with PMLD.[1]

Tim Webb's theatre company, Oily Cart, offers interactive, multi-sensory theatre to profoundly disabled children, and what is offered is an experience of smelling, hearing, touching, and feeling a rush of fanned air against your face – a world in which, as Lyn Gardner of the *Guardian* described one performance, 'soundscape, sensory diversions, colour and water come together in a liquid world of enchantment'.

The work of Oily Cart, what the performers bestow on the children, and what they succeed in bringing out of them – whether stilled attentiveness or chuckling pleasure – suggests how theatre might reveal what someone is capable of that might otherwise be thought impossible (parents watching on sometimes cannot believe their eyes); and how the subtlest enticing of the senses might draw out and enliven a previously inert and apparently 'unreachable' child.

Webb remarks: 'Some of the children have a good sense of humour. They notice incongruities. They like it when adults make a fool of themselves, or come unstuck. We might create a travelling beauty salon, and I would say that I am making this 'beauty gloop' and one of my colleagues might get up and put a big blob on my nose. And the children would find that very funny. Or we create a character, Geoff the Ref, dressed in referee's shorts, and one of us will get up and pull his shorts down, and Geoff is theatrically upset, stuttering and struggling to get his words out, and, again, the children find this very funny, perhaps even realising that Geoff wasn't really that upset.' It is of interest to watch children with no language, whose unawareness may extend to the point that they forget that they have limbs, who may sit listlessly for hours on end, and who yet chuckle when a blob of gloop is put on someone's nose, or when seeing someone's shorts pulled down. This suggests a level of awareness that might not have been anticipated; it offers, for example, evidence of some appreciation of humour, evidence which is not always entirely captured in cognitive assessments.

This point is brought out by Marjorie Clarke, Head of St Peter's School: 'We may have a whole battery of assessment tools but the biggest danger remains that we fail to recognise that a child might understand something when we hadn't realised. We have one little boy whose cognition appears to be inconsistent. If we try to get the child to recognise a ball, he can't do it. At the same time the boy gets humour. He will really laugh at some jokes.'

It is not only the striking inconsistency that deserves notice but also how humour can reveal the ability to smile, giggle, chuckle, laugh and guffaw, and, in turn, the capabilities demanded by each one of these. What is required in the way of cognition and sensibility for a child to find it funny that someone's trousers have been pulled down? At what point does she 'get the giggles', and why at that point and not another, or not at all? Neuroscience will help reveal the brain states and neural mechanisms that explain why humans have the capacities mentioned here. But there is a further aspect, about how the capacity to giggle at a joke, or smile in the presence of another, is a characteristically human expression, and what it reveals about human beings and their lives that these should be included in their expressive repertoire. We should not, however, assume that this repertoire applies to *all* humans (but then what is the significance of someone who lacks the ability to laugh or smile?), or that it applies *only* to humans, for this is to take a dogmatic view about the humour-related capacities of other animals. Yet it is worth enquiring into how some child's laughter contributes to our understanding of *him*: we recognise the smile as characteristically his, and we see by his smiling face that he is happy; the joke is an example of something that gives him the giggles and this may be different to what other children find amusing; and his personality is in part characterised by the rare or frequent response to something comical, and by how that tends to express itself, whether as a suppressed chuckle or uninhibited laughter. Theatre directors constantly make use of humour to encourage profoundly disabled children to revel in sketches that are in some way 'naughty', 'disruptive', or 'ridiculous', on the assumption that humour can help to reach people and draw them out of themselves, even in the absence of verbal communication and other basic human capabilities. Nor is it only humour and laughter that reveal comprehension and sensitivity; the capacity for sadness and grief among people with PMLD invites a similar discussion (Kittay 2005, 2009).

Spiky profiles

Educationalists use the term 'spiky profile' to refer to the unevenness of human capacities, and to underline the point that we should not assume that because someone is unable to perform well in one domain they are therefore likely not to perform well in another.

Adwoa Nyalemegbe works at the Litster School for children with severe and profound learning difficulties. Adwoa is the Ghanaian mother of Kwame, who attended the same school until he passed away, aged 15, following complications arising from pneumonia. Kwame had severe cerebral palsy, leaving him with muscle weakness, random and uncontrolled body movements, and balance and coordination problems. He had repeated seizures, and difficulties associated with drooling and swallowing. Kwame had no language, although he was able to vocalise. Mentally, however, he was 'very alert'; he had a vibrant intelligence and he needed to attend school to get over the frustration with his body. Adwoa describes her son: 'He was amazingly handsome. *Huge* expressive eyes – and he would learn to use these. He knew he was handsome – everyone told him. Amazingly, he was *so* happy – until the last few days when he was ill. When you met him you *never* felt sorry for him – *never*. He was extremely happy – he had such a great expression on his face that you didn't see his disabilities. He was such a great character.'

Whilst Kwame had no speech, he understood plenty: 'One weekend I was at home with Kwame and I was talking with his Aunt about how disabled children are treated in our home country. The services in Ghana are not good, and his Auntie had said, "They don't treat special needs children in Ghana nice." The following Monday, when I took Kwame to school he was not happy at all. Using his book – a book with pictures and photographs that I had put together with Kwame – he shared what he had learned with some of the children and teachers. I was in tears. Kwame had understood what I was discussing with his Aunt and I hadn't been sensitive to what he was capable of understanding.'

As with the children involved with Oily Cart, Kwame's intelligence was often evident in his laughter: 'His favourite TV programme was Fools and Horses – he really laughed at this until he was in tears.' Kwame was the 'biggest tease': 'His speech and language therapist would say to me: "I notice that you would bring some gadgets with you and you might bring the wrong gadget and Kwame would laugh at you." He used always to wait for me to make a mistake and the expression on his face was "Oh woman, can't you get things right!" And in class Kwame was the first to get a joke – before anybody else he would be laughing.'

In some cases the 'spikiness' of the profile is almost breathtaking. Kate is 12 years old, and has a rich, complicated and delightful personality, 'full of fun, energy and cheekiness'. She is an exceptional girl and she would not normally be included in the category of people with profound and multiple learning difficulties; yet her learning difficulties are certainly multiple and some of them are profound. She is unable to read, write or speak; she cannot wash herself, or clean her teeth, and whilst she can take herself to the bathroom she needs plenty of assistance once she is there. She is, generally, quite unable to look after herself. She is, however, mobile and has a good understanding of many words. Moreover, as her father Patrick relates, 'She has perfect pitch – and she lives for music; music is her life and soul; if you took music away from her I don't know what she would do.' Twice a week Patrick makes the 3 hour round journey for Kate's piano lesson with her teacher, James, who has known her for years: 'I love her musicianship above all else. Kate hears everything in vivid colour. At one point she would cry when listening to, say, a G7 chord. She not only hears accurately but she has a very strong emotional reaction.' So does her father, when seeing what his daughter can do: 'I love listening to her play. I record most of it. When she's here, with James, she just comes alive. And if she does something fantastic that I'd never have expected of her, it makes it all worthwhile – including those car journeys.'

Kate plays music of all kinds – this morning it is Bach and Chopin. Patrick will play a passage and Kate will follow – 'She learns by listening.' Sometimes she will play the same passage in more than one key; sometimes she will switch between Bach and Chopin; sometimes she will switch key and composer, partly for fun, partly out of mischievousness, because this makes life more difficult for Natasha who is accompanying her on the cello.

What is striking is not only Kate's musicality but her interaction with others. She and James will sometimes sit close together, Kate holding James's arm, imploring him to follow her, or looking intently into his eyes, signalling how she intends to play her next piece. She anticipates what James is expecting of her; she teases and provokes; she vocalises to her father, indicating that she wants him to clap in time to the rhythm of the music; she will cry, or scream, if James moves away from the piano stool he sometimes shares with her.

Kate is able to maintain intimate relationships and to display the complex, intentional behaviour that goes along with that. Very few children are like Kate, whether or not they have any disabilities; nor is she representative of children whose disabilities are multiple and profound, though her disabilities certainly fall into this category. I describe her here for that reason, but also so as to illustrate how uneven, unexpected, and complicated the profile of capabilities can be in one and the same person. Kate cannot brush her own teeth but she can play a Chopin prelude; she is unable to read, utter or comprehend the word 'and' but she knows a G7 chord when she hears one; she cannot participate in political decision-making, but she can initiate and engage in decisions about whether to play the music of one composer or another. Even supposing a hierarchy of capabilities, from the less to the more complex, it is not true that the ability to perform something intricate and subtle depends on an ability to perform something basic and uncomplicated. This last statement is a platitude, but it is not platitudinous when applied to people with profound learning difficulties, since it serves as a reminder that the category of 'profound disabilities' encompasses a wide variation both in ability and in people whose abilities compare favourably with others whose disabilities are less severe or who are not in any way disabled. And it is a reminder, also, that whilst a person may lack the competence to engage in political decision-making, however broadly conceived, she may have talents in other contexts that allow her to make a substantial contribution to the decisions that arise there. And this raises a question about the domains of decision-making, and the contributions appropriate to these, that should help to determine the political status of a profoundly disabled person.

'As if the clouds lifted'

The physical and cognitive capabilities of some profoundly disabled children are limited to the point that there is almost nothing that they can do unassisted, and there may be little or no progress in their functioning over long stretches of time. Teachers and carers can work for months on end without seeing any change. Here I describe a classroom session for children whose difficulties and disabilities are more extensive and profound than most children with PMLD, and I introduce one of the children, Sam, and a momentous occasion in his life.

Sam is 7 years old and is thought to be operating at the lowest of the P scales – P1, indicating the lowest level of functioning to be expected of any child in a special school.[2] He sleeps most of the time, although he will usually wake for lunch. On a good day he might rotate his head once or twice. He doesn't laugh and he doesn't smile. Daniel, his teacher, offers a stark assessment: 'Frankly, there is nothing going on and there never will be. There is no communication in anything like the ordinary sense. The only thing in a year and a half that I have ever seen Sam lift up his head for is food – this is the only motivating thing. And only particular foods – yoghurt for example. Just lifting his head in response to a favourite food is practically the only thing he does that he means something by. He won't indicate that he's hungry or that he's soiled himself … Sam just exists.'

Today Sam is in a classroom with seven children and five members of staff. The children are physically helpless: the carers initiate, support and enable almost every movement. After about 30 minutes of being massaged, one child at a time is lifted onto a blanket, held at each end by an adult, and swung gently. It is often unclear whether the child is responding to or is even aware of the words that are spoken. When it comes to Sam's turn I can see no evidence of any reaction – in his body, his face or his eyes – and he does not vocalise.

Although Sam is quiet and unresponsive, today is a 'good day'. Not so long ago he would tend to sleep almost all of the time; today he is awake, and, though quiet, he is not in any distress, and this is about as much as anyone has come to hope for. However, on one day in his life – but only one day – he responded to the sound of a bell: 'Sam vocalised, and he moved his head! No one could believe it! There wasn't a dry eye in the house! Some staff had worked with Sam for five or six years – they couldn't believe it! It was shell shock! It was, as if, just once, the clouds lifted. When his mum saw what had happened – by sheer chance we were able to film it – her face ached for smiling so much. But this hasn't happened again, though we have tried and tried.'

Today Sam is lying on the mat quietly. Very often he is slumped in his chair, eyes glazed over. Daniel reports that 'Normally you can do almost anything to Sam and you will get no response. So to see that response to the bell was really, really special.'

In the life of a young boy, who is often unresponsive, asleep, or unengaged with the world and other people, the moment when he began to vocalise and move his head in response to a ringing bell appeared to those who witnessed it as little short of a miracle. It amazed everyone who knew Sam. There will be a neurological explanation for this. But what was most significant was not so much the fleeting improvement in functioning, though that too was astonishing, but the fact of having momentarily reached Sam and watched him come alive – to see the clouds lift.

3 Making progress

Small steps

It isn't often that one will witness something as momentous as Sam's response to a bell. Far more common are slighter signs of progress – what carers often refer to as 'small steps' – which for many children would pass by without comment but which, for Alice, and her carer, both in the same class as Sam, are really worth something. Alice has no language and this morning she is not yet vocalising. She has to be moved, turned over and lifted. Eventually, and whilst lying on her stomach, she succeeds in lifting her head, and the teaching assistant is prompted to say, to no one in particular, 'She is doing really well with her head', and then, to Alice, 'Well done you, for lifting your head.' It's a little thing, but, in Alice's life, something positive and noteworthy.

The significance of taking 'little steps' is reported by Krystyna, the Polish mother of 5-year-old James: 'The best thing is when he does *small steps* at the school – for example, touching the bells by himself, or pushing the switch … *Little steps. Step by step*. We won't ever have a healthy child. But when he makes a small step it's a miracle for us.'

Even what might seem as the tiniest steps can take an age. As Veronica puts it, when talking about her 22-year-old daughter Harriet, some children have a different rhythm: 'Harriet always has the potential to develop but the steps along the way are *minute … progress is so slow*. Moving from taking 5 seconds to brush her teeth to spending 5 seconds brushing one side of her mouth, then 5 seconds brushing the other, and then not throwing the tooth brush away. And progress on this scale might take 9 months, 12 months even. Harriet has a different rhythm. The goal of this year is that Harriet should learn to clean her teeth and not throw her tooth brush away.'

Not throwing the toothbrush away: something that might pass without mention; but for Harriet, and her parents, a significant achievement.

'You've got to want to get them'

The determination that a child should make progress can require an act of faith, religious or otherwise (see Chapter 8). Patricia Simons is an experienced teacher of children with profound learning difficulties at Elisabeth Beasley School in south-east England: 'You've got to believe that there is more there – because there is. These children are on an incredibly long journey. You absolutely *never* say never. No matter how low functioning, all children have their likes and dislikes, their favourite positions, smells, sounds, people.'

Such unshakeable belief is typically accompanied by an intense commitment to the children themselves. Patricia puts it like this: 'You have to like children. Of course, you have to be a watcher, an observer. But you also have to respond with emotion; *you've got to want to get them*. I want to understand what makes the children in my class happy.' And to do that 'You have to be comfortable in your skin – happy to lie on the floor going "ba, ba, ba". And you've got not to mind snot and smells and bodily fluids. You can't mind much what you look like either – I mean, you have to be prepared to make a bit of a fool of yourself.' Patricia doesn't like the word 'patience': 'That's not the right word. It's about *expectation* – I expect that these children will take a long, long time to show me stuff.'

She gives the example of 5-year-old Zidan who has complex physical difficulties, low muscle tone and a lot of uncontrolled movement. He is currently learning to separate from his mother and father, and for a long time 'he cried pretty much all morning, every morning. We changed his chair, so that his arm was no longer getting stuck and he no longer banged his head. We discovered that, if we relieved any physical discomfort in his hips, and we took him out of his chair with a routine he got used to, he gradually began to cry less. And we realised that this was about both reducing his pain and his knowing what to expect. It took six months to see a grin! In the early days it was only a "Mona Lisa" [i.e. faint] smile; but as he got used to us, as we got the chair right, as we got the routine right, we eventually came to see a great big open mouthed smile – it goes all the way up to his eyes!'

It doesn't quite always work out. Very occasionally Patricia reaches an impasse, as with Jack, who is quadriplegic: 'There was something about the way he looked at you. We truly believed that in there was a cognitively able child – if only we could just unlock him. Signing aids were very difficult for him. All of us were convinced that if we found the right aid we would unlock him. But we never did; we never could. It was his gaze – he would gaze really intently. Everyone who knew him felt that there was so much locked inside.'

Toileting and sexuality

Very few parents are prepared to be quite as open and honest as Jo. When talking about her 14-year-old profoundly disabled son Alex, she spoke candidly about two intimate subjects: toileting and sexuality. For Alex, as for his parents, who had to cope with him 'smearing poo all over the walls', to progress from 'smearing shit on the walls to wiping his own bum' represented enormous progress; 'and everything that Alex has achieved, this included, we've worked with him 100 per cent'. Many parents will understand that very well, including Sally, who talked about how much effort went into helping her son Paul to learn how to manage himself when toileting: 'Oh my God – what it took to get him to toilet himself!' From 'smearing' to not smearing; from not smearing to wiping oneself – this much progress represents several huge steps in the lives of some children and their families.

Whilst it is not unusual for parents to discuss toileting, not many are prepared to talk about sexuality. Jo talks about how vulnerable her son Alex is, and how she has had to teach him to live with his sexuality, although he has only a limited understanding of privacy and of what we would think of as 'appropriate' sexual behaviour: 'You worry about sexual abuse. He sort of knows that his willy is private but he doesn't know what privacy means. So he doesn't really know that his willy is private. He could be abused by a paedophile. He's a sitting duck, like a lot of the children. He has no concept of privacy.'

Alex has sexual impulses similar to many boys of his age; in that respect his functioning is nothing out of the ordinary. But his understanding is such that he not only has no concept of privacy but 'He will never have a relationship – it's not at that level.' That leaves Jo teaching Alex how to respond to sexual desire in the privacy of his bedroom: 'If he's outside and his hands go down his pants I say, "Ah – to your bedroom! – It's OK to play with your willy *in your bedroom*." It took us a long time to get there. I wish I had been able to prepare him for puberty. It took a while, and with understanding it became easier. We bought a toy, something that looked like a willy – and if he put his hands down his pants in public I'd give him his willy toy and I'd say "You can play with that." They start young and they don't have shame like other kids.'

Alex's sexual functioning is not unusual, but his cognitive functioning is. When the discrepancy is particularly large, there are special challenges in the way of enabling a person to learn how to get to know and look after themselves. And that is not only a challenge for parents and carers: as Jo says, 'On sex, this is something that the school needs to talk about more.'

Living with a degenerative condition

Some children live with a degenerative condition which prevents them from developing their capabilities, or, at least, from sustaining any development for long periods. Grace is a 5-year-old girl with a degenerative condition who attends St Peter's School. She is visually impaired and hearing impaired, and she has an intervener who helps her to interpret the world, and other people to interpret and understand her. Grace often makes significant progress, but periodically there is a deterioration in her health, and that leaves Marjorie, the head teacher, with a problem: 'On the one hand we want to encourage Grace to achieve new things but every six months or so we will be set back a bit – not exactly back to Square 1, but it definitely takes us back a few steps. But then Grace often surprises us and bounces back more than we tend to expect.'

The most important thing, as far as Marjorie is concerned, is 'not just having our own agenda, but learning from the child and learning to take small steps based on our close observations of Grace. If Grace can tolerate standing, with support, for 5 minutes then the school might extend that so that the aim is to stand for 6 minutes.' But there are times when Marjorie is faced with a choice between two priorities: on the one hand, encouraging children to learn and to develop; on the other, allowing them to stay with what is familiar and most comfortable, 'It feels right to challenge our children, reasonably and comfortably. But if I'm working with a child with an extremely complex disorder, or with a degenerative disorder, and perhaps she is coming to the end of her life, then our aims are very much about contentment and enjoyment.'

Promoting personal autonomy – pupils' learning and capabilities – is perhaps the single most important value in the professional outlook of most teachers and educationalists. What are schools for if not to challenge and encourage their pupils to grow and develop? But there may come a point when it is no longer possible for a child to grow any further: perhaps the degeneration is too far advanced; or, even if it is *possible* to encourage some development, it may not be *worth* the effort – the price is too high, the struggle too great, to allow us to do anything other than provide for the safest and most comfortable life that we can manage. When the ideals of promoting autonomy and wellbeing push in different directions we come up against an enduring conflict between our basic values. This conflict is sometimes present in the world of profound disability, leaving practitioners and carers with a series of what are often acutely painful and difficult decisions.

'No one is ineducable'

Phillippa Cauldwell is a Multi-sensory Specialist at Mayfield School, a special school for secondary-aged children with severe and profound learning difficulties. Phillippa is adamant that no one is ineducable. She acknowledges that, for the child who is functioning at the very lowest levels, it might take five years before she succeeds in prompting much in the way of a response. But even then, '*You are moving towards them, opening the world out to them.*' She gives an example of how the world opened out for one young man, the 'most physically and mentally disabled man I've met in 20 years. He was *so* ill that we didn't make transition plans. He wasn't going to make it. He was incredibly passive. He might roll his eyes but even then the intent was unclear. So I made a CD to include various pieces of music – about eight tracks – Yo Yo Ma playing Bach, some Heart FM tracks – Take That – and something from Count Basie. I played these tracks in class, over and over, for a term. And by the end of that term he started vocalising and flaring his nostrils in what looked like an angry response to the classical music! Within another half term the corners of his mouth would turn up to Take That. We were just thrilled because it became consistent. So we swapped the order of the tracks around, and he had the same response to the same tracks, though they now appeared in a different order. From the look on his face, and the way his body stiffened, we could see that he didn't like the classical music and he did like Take That!'

This experience was used as a 'gateway': 'From there, if he didn't like something – say, something tactile – he had some control and it was fabulous.' Phillippa insists that '*anyone* is educable. I don't think it's impossible to reach anybody. I just don't think I have all the tools to know how to do it.'

Not that Phillippa pretends that it's easy. She believes that music touches the soul, and her task is to find the right music to do that. But how to be sure of success? On watching one child listening to Yo Yo Ma, Phillippa had noted that he looked 'visibly relaxed', whilst another colleague had written that he looked 'bored'. There are difficulties of interpretation here that Phillippa would acknowledge; there are times when it is possible to do no more than offer a 'best guess', arrived at after considering several possible readings of someone's behaviour.

Patricia Simons is familiar with having to rely upon a best collective guess: 'Sometimes we have to try and work out what the different types of crying, or facial movements or body gestures might mean. Sometimes we really don't know what to think. Or it can turn out that the most unlikely thing is what matters. We had a child who was sometimes happy, sometimes distressed. After weeks and weeks of observation, it turned out that it all had to do with where the teacher's feet were lying! If the teacher's feet lay within the squares on the carpet it was OK; but if her feet lay on more than one square, or on a border between one and another, it was not OK. It took a very long time to work that out!'

Sheila Evans, Deputy Head of Mayfield School, acknowledges that it can be difficult to interpret the behaviour of some of the most profoundly disabled children in her school. She encourages her staff to 'treat behaviour as if it is intentional with the aim of making it so'. With some of her pupils who are at 'very early levels of development', the response of teachers is often 'very personal and hard to justify with solid evidence'. She is well aware that some children at her school won't have the ability to recognise any one particular teacher, and might not notice if one teacher left and another took their place. But of one thing she is firmly convinced: 'There is no child who cannot respond to another human being who treats them properly. I haven't come across a child for whom this is not the case. There may be children who, when they are very sick, do not manage to respond to others. But when they are well they do respond. And we've never had a child who can't make a connection, given the right support.' Sheila is adamant that 'the thing that makes the most difference to children's lives is the *quality of their relationships*'. Moreover: 'It is a matter of amazement to me that all profoundly disabled children can be *active* partners in a relationship. I see these children all the time 'holding' the adults – what they do affects the adults' behaviour, in the same way that young babies affect their parents.' In over 32 years of teaching, Sheila insists that there is no child for whom her schools have not been able to nurture a relationship that is worthwhile, meaningful, and life enhancing.

4 P scales and the school curriculum

Any discussion of human capabilities should look at how these are documented and assessed in the school curriculum for children with PMLD, and this takes us to the subject of P scales, although there is not space to consider either the curriculum or the P scales in any detail.[3] The experience of working with P scales will vary from one teacher and one school to another; the significance of the testimony presented below is less to provide evidence of how P scales are used in schools – a subject I can only dip into – and more to illustrate some general issues pertaining to capabilities that are likely to arise whenever they are applied to children with PMLD. We hear from three head or deputy head teachers: Marjorie Clarke, Sheila Evans and Penny Robinson, who, between them, have experience of working in special schools which extends to over 70 years.

Marjorie Clarke is Head of St Peter's School, which caters for a wide range of learning difficulties and disabilities, including 19 children, aged between 2 and 11, whose difficulties are multiple and profound. St Peter's School was recently awarded 'outstanding' grades in all departments following an Ofsted Inspection. Almost all the children at St Peter's make outstanding progress; however, the children who tend to make least progress are those with PMLD. Marjorie considers that she, the school, and Ofsted are only just beginning to understand the world as experienced by these children.

Evidence used in inspections raises a question about how best to gauge and assess the learning progress made by children with profound learning difficulties. Are P scales sufficiently sensitive to allow for the fine distinctions it is necessary to take account of in this context? P scales are descriptions of attainment levels below Level 1 of the National Curriculum, and they describe the knowledge, skill and understanding that children gain from each of the subjects they study. There are eight levels, P1 to P8 for each subject, including the core subjects of English, Maths, Science and Personal, Social and Health Education (PSHE). When, in the past, teachers reported that for children with PMLD it was very difficult to make progress through even the lowest P levels, each of Levels 1–3 was split into two, as in P1(i) and P1(ii), for example. Here are two examples of descriptions of performance in English – the first, P1(i), at the lowest end of the P scales, the second, P2(ii), at a higher level:

> P1(i). Pupils encounter activities and experiences. They may be passive or resistant. They may show simple reflex responses, for example, startling at sudden noises or movements. Any participation is fully prompted.
>
> P2(ii). Pupils begin to be proactive in their interactions. They communicate consistent preferences and affective responses, for example, reaching out to a favourite person. They recognise familiar people, events and objects, for example, vocalising or gesturing in a particular way in response to a favourite visitor. They perform actions, often by trial and improvement, and they remember learned responses over short periods of time, for example, showing pleasure each time a particular puppet character appears in a poem dramatized with sensory cues. They cooperate with shared exploration and supported participation, for example, taking turns in interaction with a familiar person, imitating actions and facial expressions.
>
> *(Department for Education 2014: 11)*

It will be evident how great is the distance between P1(i) and P2(ii). It is, at any rate, to Marjorie: 'The P1–P2 levels are not sufficiently accurate or discriminating. Ofsted use guidance from the Department of Education (2010), and the DfE expects progress from P1(i) to P2(ii) – that is to expect too much! Anyone who made so much progress would be a completely different child – all the way from P1(i) to P2(ii) by the end of Key Stage 2!'[4]

This is not to deny that a child can make impressive progress, and sometimes so much that it is no longer obvious that he should continue to learn in a group with other children with multiple and profound disabilities. Marjorie describes one boy who was beginning to cry when his mother and father left him at school, who put his fingers in his ears as a sign that he was anticipating what was coming next, and who began to engage in simple ICT programmes. When watching television he followed movements on the screen, whilst other children simply listened and were very still, and this same boy is now beginning to express his likes and dislikes. Marjorie has to ask herself whether it is now time for him to move to a different class, and a case such as this is by no means unique.

Marjorie maintains that the descriptive levels used in many assessment tools are often too few and too simple: 'We just assume that this is what PMLD children will like, because other children do. But how do we know? We need to know more.' St Peter's opted to make use of an additional instrument which identifies 40 areas of activity, and which takes as a starting point the need to identify activities that the children are actually able to undertake: 'For example, we look at whether they can track from left to right. If so, can they track both in semi-darkness and in a well-lit environment? In this way we seek to build up a picture of what they *can* do, rather than what they are *unable* to do. We find that teachers and parents prefer this approach. So we place much more emphasis on observation and on allowing time to understand what children can learn, as distinct from teaching skills to children. This gives us a better picture of who the children are and what they are capable of.'

Progress may be so gradual as to require considerable skill and a refined instrument to do justice to it. Time and perseverance are necessary too: 'When we look at the achievements of the children we find that they may acquire one or two of these skills at the end of a year, but only following constant, consistent and focused high-quality teaching. And this level of progress is not even close to the equivalent of moving from one P level to the next.'

For progress of this kind to be achieved, teachers must use the same language and routines over and over again in order to allow children to understand what they are being encouraged to do: 'It's about us *being consistent in our responses* – our children may then have more control over how they express themselves and respond.'

Marjorie has concluded that 'We need to put less emphasis on teaching skills for learning and more on allowing learners to teach us. We need both, of course, but we need more of the second, so that we can learn from our children about what they need and how they prefer to or are able to learn best.'

Sheila Evans, Deputy Head of Mayfield School, agrees. Mayfield is one of the larger schools that cater to children with special educational needs, including children with multiple and profound learning difficulties. Sheila arrived at Mayfield 32 years ago, and she observes that in the late 1980s there was a need to develop an alternative to the national curriculum, which was not then designed with the children at Mayfield in mind. Like other pioneering teachers working in schools for children with PMLD (see Hobbs 2014), Sheila describes the curriculum that she helped to develop as 'bottom up and developmental'. Moreover: 'If you get the curriculum right at the earliest stages, there shouldn't be a distinction between what a child enjoys and the activities necessary for them to learn.' Sheila emphasises that children need 'to be able to communicate, to be confident, to understand the experiences they are having in the *here and now*. For many of our children, their lives are *of the moment*. A lot of what we teach is that if you do something now, there will be an effect later, but to begin with you have to work within *a ridiculously short time-scale* – perhaps 5 seconds, or 10 minutes – but *not* "next week".'

It is essential that curriculum materials are directly relevant to children's experiences. The tasks that teachers give to children should be intrinsically rewarding, and to be sure that they are, teachers have to be 'unrelenting in analysing what it is that a child is experiencing and learning'. Any episode of learning has to be put into a context that will *mean* something – for example, the context provided by the celebration of Christmas. Of course, the children don't know what Christmas is or what it represents; they don't have the concepts or the level of understanding that would allow them to grasp that. What is required is 'to provide a sensory world, full of bright, interesting things that excite, that feel good, that are worth reaching out for, and which are all associated with the magic of Christmas – and the children will respond to some of the 'magic', even if 'Christmas' doesn't mean a great deal to them.'

Above all, what matters most to Sheila is 'reaching a child *now*, and getting her to realise how interesting the world can be. I keep coming back to the importance of a curriculum that will improve the quality of a child's life *now*. "How are your senses to understand the world now?" Because it's an interesting place now – and your life will be better if you take an interest in life around you, as opposed to having your head down in your lap.'

Penny Robinson, Head of Elisabeth Beasley School, would endorse every word of this last paragraph. 'I had a child at this school who died last week. What I want to know is that this child had a good time at school, enjoyed himself, was interested in life; not that she had good P-levels. Even for the children who would be categorised as "life-limited" I want to know that they have had a fabulous time.'

But Penny would also acknowledge that the introduction of P-levels can encourage teachers to think positively: 'What the P-levels do is help teachers think about what we do. What I want for my children, more than anything else, is that they have a fulfilling life, an exciting life. But what these initiatives do – the national curriculum, P-levels – is encourage us to think about the opportunities we offer them. There is a talented bunch of practitioners in special schools – very good at thinking creatively about whatever comes their way. But following the national curriculum, using P-levels, I learned to see that there were more possibilities – in science education, to take just one example – than I had realised before.'

Sheila, Marjorie and Penny are just three of many experienced teachers who have worked to implement a curriculum that is best suited to encouraging the development of children with profound and multiple learning difficulties. The emphasis on learning from pupils, and on relevance, immediacy, patience, 'small steps', multi-sensory stimulation and intensive interaction between teacher and learner can be found in numerous special schools. These schools seek to recognise the distinctive capabilities of children with PMLD, and the corresponding need for a curriculum that is sensitive to that, including the fine grained and subtle judgements that any appreciation of the children's capabilities and progress will require.

I can do no more than touch on the subject of a curriculum for children with PMLD; it deserves an extensive discussion to itself, in order to do justice to the many inspiring innovations and approaches that have been developed in recent years, and in each of the cognitive, sensory, communicative, physical and caring domains. Fortunately, there are many books given over entirely to this subject.[5]

5 Concluding remarks

Whilst there is a group of people who can be categorised as having multiple and profound learning difficulties and disabilities, we should recognise the great variety in the levels of functioning and capabilities that this group encompasses: as between one person and another; within one and the same person depending on which of their capabilities we are looking at; and between what a person is capable of today and what she might be capable of in a month, or in six months, or a year. Of course, profoundly disabled children will tend to have fewer and often much less well developed capabilities than most other children. It is not helpful, and not in anyone's interests, to deny this as a general rule. Yet, there are exceptions: Kate is one (and how many more children are there like Kate?). And, much more important, the general rule doesn't take us very far: it doesn't encourage us to do what Marjorie, Sheila, Penny and other teachers and carers who work with children with PMLD are so adept at doing: understanding the distinctive life and profile of each individual child, appreciating how each is best encouraged to develop, and working at a pace and towards a goal that is manageable and comfortable for them. Above all, it doesn't encourage us to recognise what people with PMLD *are* capable of, including the fundamental human capacity to give and receive love and affection; nor what it can *mean* to a child, and to those who care for him, to stand for 6 minutes rather than 5, to push a switch by himself, to lift his head whilst lying on a mat – even to respond to a bell. To appreciate what someone with PMLD is capable of, and the significance of their progress and achievements, requires not only an understanding of the person gained from extensive first-hand experience, but also a preparedness to look for signs of their responsiveness and potential, and to go on (and on) looking; all of which takes us a long way beyond any initial categorisation of their capabilities as absent, limited or underdeveloped.

Points for discussion

- How helpful is it to think about a child in terms of their capabilities? What could be missed out by looking only at what a child is capable of?
- Have you ever seriously underestimated what a child with PMLD can do? What did you miss, and why?
- How do you manage to make the most of children's capabilities whilst also showing understanding of what they find most difficult or distressing?
- Are children who live with a degenerative or life-limiting condition a special case? Should we think about how to develop their capabilities differently from how we think about other children?

Notes

1 Much of the work of Oily Cart takes place in schools, and it is to this context that the evidence on participating children applies.
2 For more on P scales see section 4 of this chapter.

3   For extended discussion see Ndaji and Tymms 2009; for discussion of learning programmes for children with PMLD see Hogg and Sebba 1986; and for a recent insightful assessment of curricula for children with PMLD, including a detailed review of the Profound Education Curriculum and of the materials used in 12 special schools, see Hobbs 2014.
4   The National Curriculum is organised into 'blocks' of years, called Key Stages, and Key Stage 2 applies to children aged between 7 and 11.
5   See, to take just three recent examples, Imray and Hinchcliffe 2013; Colley 2013; Longhorn 2010.

3

HUMAN CAPABILITIES

In theory

1 Introduction

Having explored a few of the capabilities of people with profound disabilities I shall now take a look at how philosophers refer to human capabilities in their accounts of what all human beings need in order to have a life worth living, and what, fundamentally, all human beings are entitled to.

Human capabilities comprise all the capabilities that we either have or might develop: this includes not only what we can actually do now, but also what we could do if we had a choice, or if we were provided with a suitable opportunity. The emphasis is on our potential as human beings: on what we are capable of, or would be capable of if we are well cared for and actively encouraged, and if we, and those who care for us, are given the resources that allow us to develop to the best of our ability.

Philosophers have written extensively about human capabilities, some, indeed, suggesting that capabilities should figure at the centre of any theory of justice. The two best-known advocates of 'capability theory' are Amartya Sen and Martha Nussbaum. In section 2, I examine the role of freedom in Sen's work as a value for assessing the condition of human beings. In section 3 I explore some remarks by Nussbaum on how we should regard capabilities for the purpose of determining our political entitlements. And in section 4 I consider whether the language of capability theory will capture all of what is most precious and valuable about people with profound disabilities.

This chapter can only serve as a brief, partial and introductory exploration of capability theory. The aim is both to indicate why the theory is important for anyone who wishes to think about profound disability and to point up a number of significant limitations and points of controversy.

2 Freedom

Freedom is at the centre of Sen's account of capability: capability reflects the 'person's freedom to lead one type of life or another', and capability to achieve functionings 'constitute the person's freedom – the real opportunities – to have wellbeing' (Sen 1992: 40, 49). The category of capabilities is well suited to reflect the ideal of freedom of action since 'capability to function reflects what a person *can* do' (Sen 1984: 317). The concept of capability is a 'freedom type notion' and the functionings available to a person determine her '*well-being freedom*' (Sen 1985: 201). 'This freedom, reflecting a person's opportunities of well-being, must be valued at least for *instrumental* reasons ... but in addition ... freedom may be seen as being intrinsically important for a good social structure. A good society, in this view, is also a society of freedom' (Sen 1992: 41).

The centrality of freedom is evident in Terzi's application of capability to disability. Under the capability approach the distinction between the biological and social causes of disability assumes less significance than in some rival accounts, since we are directed to attend to 'the full set of capabilities a person can choose from and the role impairment plays in this set of freedoms' (Terzi 2010: 91). The emphasis in capability theory is not 'actual achieved functionings but the effective access to the achievement of these functionings' (Terzi 2007: 763). Burchardt concurs, recommending that we consider not only a person's functionings but also her capabilities:

> [T]he freedom to achieve a functioning ... may be valued even if the individual does not at present wish to do so ... Thus someone who has limited opportunities in this and other respects can be identified as disadvantaged ... without imposing any standard of normality or overriding his or her own preferences ... Liberation from disability is about having choices, not about living life in conformity to some pre-defined notion of normality.
>
> *(2004: 742)*

It is not in doubt that freedom and autonomy number among the most important values in any human life, whoever we are, whatever our disabilities. And these values are affirmed by everyone, or almost everyone who teaches and otherwise works with profoundly disabled people. The overriding goal, very often, is just the promotion of independence and the related freedoms – especially freedom of movement, action and choice. Some of the most inspiring stories to be related in this book include people who have managed to acquire and to exercise more freedom and independence than would have been thought possible, whether because they can now toilet themselves, interact with a computer or live away from home in protected accommodation.

However, this emphasis on freedom and choice is not always helpful in identifying what is of basic importance for profoundly disabled people. To start with an example: it is not always possible to know what a person wants, including on matters of health and nutrition. If we do not know whether a person wants her soiled nappy changed, and she risks infection if we don't change it, then we should change it, since we have as an over-arching aim her good health and cleanliness. In this case a person's good health is a consideration in our decision-making not only because, or even principally because, it represents the value of freedom.

We can distinguish: (1) maintaining good health; (2) maintaining good health when but not because this conforms to what you would have wanted; and (3) maintaining good health because this is what you want. (3) represents an example in which you exercise freedom of choice. If (1) and (2) obtain, then, whilst your health is preserved and that is what you want, your counterfactual preference is not a reason for the outcome. Perhaps only (1) obtains. The preference is for the nappy to stay; the wearer prefers the warm sensation of a soiled nappy to the alternative, and she prefers that because, in an environment of few stimuli, this sensation stands out not only as pleasant but also as one which occupies her attention. These two reasons are enough to make this decision less easy than it might appear, but it may yet be the right thing to change the nappy. If that is what we do, though the wearer requests that we do not, then what we do is for her own good, although it is neither in conformity with her will, nor undertaken, therefore, because it is her will.

Perhaps we too hastily conclude that what we do in (3) is to secure a basic good for the nappy wearer. There yet remains a distinction between what is good for her, what conforms to her will, and what conforms to her will because it is her will, and the present point is that *all three* aspects pertain to our assessment of what we should do. What is good for someone may be obtained independently of or in spite of their will, and, therefore, in the absence of any exercise of freedom on their part. Typically, whatever conforms to our will is also what we would have aimed at had we exercised any freedom of our own. But what we would have aimed at may yet be good for us, even though, as a matter of fact, it did not issue from our will. And this consideration, which is not a freedom-related consideration, is pertinent to the lives of profoundly disabled people. When taking decisions on behalf of other people, or deciding on the resources that they are entitled to, we should be responsive to the provision of goods and options that the exercise of free choice is typically aimed at but is not always involved in (cf. Cohen 2011: 71–80).

The value of freedom does not serve to draw attention to the entire range of basic human functioning. Because not all valuable functioning is related to agency, it is not always pertinent to look at whether a child with cerebral palsy should choose to be suctioned, even if the option of suctioning is included in the capability set she is free to access. What matters is that she should be suctioned by a trained parent or professional. An assessment of the condition of profoundly disabled children should look less at whether they can choose a loving family and more on whether they belong to such a family; less on the opportunity to achieve healthy and secure emotional attachments and more on their being healthy and emotionally secure (Macleod 2010: 185). The value of these goods is not – or not only – their contribution to the development of the ability to make choices.

3 Entitlement and political status

I turn now to Martha Nussbaum, and take notice of how she invokes the concept of capabilities in her 'capabilities approach' to a theory of justice. A distinguishing feature of her work is a proposal that human dignity can serve as the basis of an entitlement to an extensive set of capabilities that *all* human beings either possess or have the potential to develop. This is an inspiring vision: no one is left outside the ambit of a conception of justice which is responsive to the needs and dependencies of even the most vulnerable humans.

Human dignity includes a life that has available in it 'truly human functioning' (Nussbaum 2006: 74), and Nussbaum identifies the central human capabilities as these apply to life, bodily health, bodily integrity and other essential dimensions of a worthwhile human life (ibid.: 76–78). These are conceived in terms of 'what people are actually able to do and to be, in a way informed by an intuitive idea of a life that is worthy of the dignity of a human being' (ibid.: 70). The basic idea is that, by imagining a life without the capability in question, that life would not be worthy of human dignity (ibid.: 78). The capabilities are to be pursued for every person, and there is a threshold for each capability, beneath which 'truly human functioning' is not possible.

Nussbaum is insistent that the same minimum threshold for the same set of political entitlements should apply to all citizens:

> [T]he political entitlements of all citizens are equal and the same ... if we say anything else, we fail to respect people with disabilities as fully equal citizens. To say that this person will have property rights and that one will not, that this one will be able to vote and that one will not, seems an intolerable violation of *equal* respect for human dignity.
>
> *(2008: 363)*

One reason for the insistence is that 'if we start fashioning different levels of political entitlement we lose a strong incentive ... for making every effort we can to develop the capacities of people with disabilities to the point at which they are able to exercise these entitlements on their own' (2008: 363–364). There is a tendency to underestimate the potential of people with learning difficulties, owing to ignorance, prejudice or a disinclination to meet the cost of providing adequate support. This tendency to 'construct failure' applies in particular to people with cognitive impairments, as when the prejudice that children with Down's syndrome were ineducable prevented an accurate appraisal of what they were capable of achieving. Nussbaum is one of many capability theorists who need no reminding of this. She proposes that we work 'tirelessly to bring all children with disabilities up to the threshold of capability that we set for other citizens' (2006: 190).

This strategy is not shown to be unjustified merely because we can identify persons who do not meet the threshold. There may be good reason to proceed 'as if everyone was capable of all the major capabilities' (2008: 362) just because, although some people may not meet the threshold now, they may yet be enabled to, and nothing less than unqualified support, practical and political, will suffice to overcome the obstacles, including discrimination and prejudice, that now stand in their way.

At the same time it is one thing to proceed as if a person has a capacity when, though lacking it now, she may attain it in the future, and another if a person is not now capable and it is likely or certain that she never will be. What is the position for profoundly disabled people who, after all our efforts, are unable to attain some of the central capabilities? Nussbaum stands firm: 'Here I insist that they still have these capabilities, for example the right to vote and the right to own property; but that these capabilities in some cases will have to be exercised in a relationship with a guardian' (2008: 364). Nussbaum writes illuminatingly about guardianship in connection with political entitlement (2006: 195–199; 2009: 343–350) but the point here is to notice the suggested extension to how we conceive capabilities: we may regard a person as having a capability if though she lacks it now, she may attain it in the future; and we may take a similar view if though she will always lack it when acting alone, she may possess it when acting with others.

We will want to distinguish between cases in which I make decisions on my own behalf and those in which, with support and guidance, I am enabled to reveal preferences so as to inform a decision made by my guardian. But Nussbaum is right to consider a conception of 'capability' that is not confined to current and unassisted effort, and to pursue the moral and political implications of capabilities whose realisation is dependent on the assistance of others. Indeed, it is one purpose of maintaining a single list of capabilities that it should raise 'all these questions, and they are vital ones, if people with mental impairments and disabilities are to be fully equal as citizens' (2006: 194–195).

Some of these questions, however, only serve to draw attention to the many demands being put upon the concept of 'capability'; it is beginning to look as if a degree of elasticity is required that leaves it unclear as to where the boundaries of the concept are to be found. There is a sense in which I have the capability of feeding myself even though I cannot feed myself but must rely on the assistance of my carer, who spoon feeds me (in this case, I can actively help and indicate my preferences); but this is not the same sense of capability that applies if my carer does not spoon food me but, rather, ensures safe intravenous ingestion as the only reliable means of nourishment for someone who is unable to move their limbs or comprehend the actions and choices associated with being fed (here, there is the requisite level of functioning, but I am unable to provide any assistance). And what is the sense in which I have the capacity to vote if, though I have a guardian to act in my best interests, I have never exhibited understanding of any words, images or symbols which might be used to elicit a preference relating to my voting options? In this case, is there *any* aspect of functioning that we can identify that applies specifically to the capacity to vote? This is to ask about how treating someone as having a set of capabilities is sensitive to their cognitive functioning, dependency on assistance and on any expression of agency; and how far capability is a product not only of current capacity, however augmented, but of predicted future capacity. And this in turn raises questions about how any judgement of capability admits of, or demands, a set of counterfactual judgements, and how ambitious these can intelligibly be.

DiSilvestro pursues counter-factual lines of enquiry more vigorously than most, arguing that if we 'can *conceivably* heal [some] individual this shows that they still have certain capacities, and it's the fact that they have these capacities that gives them moral status' (2010: 198, my italics). He suggests, for example, that the possibilities associated with 'futuristic hypothetical technology' permit us to consider an anencephalic infant as 'a human organism with the higher-order capacity to think' (ibid.: 196). As he concedes, however, it is, to say the least, a 'significant stretch' to see how we should supply any content to this claim. Anencephaly is characterised by a congenital absence of most of the brain and the presence of only a rudimentary brain stem. It follows as a matter of definition that no one person can both be anencephalic and have the capacity for thought. There is in any case no existing or proposed medical intervention that would have the effect of providing an anencephalic infant with the capacity to think; nor, even supposing the development of some 'futuristic' technology, do we have any adequate specification of one and the same person who has been anencephalic and who later comes to develop the said capacity.

We should acknowledge that 'higher-order thought' is not a capability that applies to all human beings, including anencephalic human beings alive today. No matter how generous our estimation, there must come a point at which we can no longer treat a child as if he has capabilities similar to those of other children, for otherwise any amount of lack of functioning is compatible with an assertion of capability, and this is incoherent.

Nor need any such acknowledgement have the unwelcome political implications that Nussbaum warns against; for we have other conceptual materials at our disposal, and these may be called into service in an effort to protect the condition and status of those profoundly disabled persons whose capabilities and functionings are conspicuous by their absence. Scanlon is just one of many philosophers for whom *what we have good reason to want* is fundamental to understanding what we owe to each other. He explicitly considers the case of humans who never develop the capacity for judgement-sensitive attitudes, and he, like DiSilvestro, invokes a counter-factual possibility:

> the idea of justifiability to them must be understood counterfactually, in terms of what they could reasonably reject if they were able to understand … a question [about what they have good reason to want].
>
> *(2000: 185).*

A person may have a good reason not to want to be left slumped in a wheelchair for hours on end, even if there are times when she does not realise what is wrong with that, or that she might have been given better options. We should allow that capability is sometimes absent, whilst at the same time insisting that someone may yet be owed what is best for her, and 'owed' because this is what justice requires.

This discussion has brought out two difficulties: it is unlikely that one and the same concept of capability can be applied to the entire range of cases mentioned here; and in some instances it is far from obvious that any concept of capability will serve as the basis for all the claims of justice we would want to make on behalf of people with profound disabilities.

4 Capability and contribution

To conclude this chapter I wish to explore the connection between what people are able to contribute and what they are capable of. Is everything that a person contributes – to others, and to the world – always best captured by the language of capabilities?

Whilst the children that Oily Cart work with may never participate in politics or in any form of decision-making, they might succeed – and for the Director, Tim Webb, they *do* succeed – in contributing to a theatrical event, becoming members of a group sharing in a common human endeavour. We are shown how a human being may surprise herself, and us, when brought alive by something captivating, becoming part of a spectacle that she will not see for herself but which she is yet participating in and representing. This is an example of participation that any capability 'audit' ought to take notice of, as a contribution to a communal exercise, however modest and curtailed. Nor is the contribution entirely to be explained in terms of individual functioning: there is a collective aspect to a group performance, a relational aspect to the good humoured interaction, and the significance of the spectacle as a whole – which includes what the children reveal themselves to be capable of in their own right, certainly, and also as members of a group, which, as a group, is responsible for a charming piece of theatre.

We should, at least, insist that any account of contribution acknowledge the significance of what an individual can give to others. Pamela is the mother of George, her profoundly disabled 6-year-old boy, who has no language, is registered blind, experiences daily seizures, and is unable to move his head, hands or body unaided. Despite this, Pamela insists that George is a very happy little child: 'He always has a smile on his face. Everybody we meet, they just fall in love with him. When we came to the school, all the teachers were saying, "I want him in my class!" Maybe it's just his little face.' More than anything: 'I enjoy George's company. And I need him as much as he needs me. I owe him everything. George has made me appreciate life – the slightest little thing in life. I appreciate life more now.'

The difficulty of establishing capabilities, and the relation between capabilities and contribution, are highlighted by Fiona, talking about her 14-year-old son, Richard: 'You can never know, you can never know. Someone who does not know Richard might think that he can only do a tenth of the things he can actually do. It depends on how you value your life. It's so brutal to say, "Your functioning is limited." Richard has such a capacity for enjoyment – he really does enjoy his life – he has a good time – he wants to be here. And when he is enjoying himself he lights up the world around him. He draws the best out of other people. We live in a small community. The men who run the coffee shop – they love him. When he smiles everyone smiles.'

The ability to be nice to people, to be happy and to make others happy, to love and inspire love: any taxonomy should do justice to these basic human capabilities, acknowledging their contribution to what we value, in other people, in relationships, in communities. At the same time, if it is capabilities of this kind that also serve to secure someone's political status – as a person with rights and as having the status of a citizen – we will need to explain why it is that these particular capabilities have the political implications that they do, including when other basic capabilities are absent.

This leads on to a final question, about how far what we owe people is dependent on their capabilities, however broadly these are conceived. When Pamela was asked what was so special about her son George, there was a long pause before she said simply, 'It's … just him … just him.' This calls to mind some words of Simone Weil: 'I see a passer by in the street. He has long arms, blue eyes and a mind whose thoughts I do not know, but perhaps they are commonplace.' She asks what it is about him that is 'sacred' to her, and answers: 'It is he. The whole of him. The arms, the eyes, the thoughts, everything' (2005: 70–71).

Watching George one morning in a classroom, lying helpless on a mat whilst his body was massaged by a carer, who all the while talks tenderly to him, treating him as someone precious, though his body is unresponsive and he appears not to understand much if anything of what is said, one is prompted to ask whether Pamela and Weil have said something important; about whether what we value is a response not only to someone's characteristics, notable or commonplace, but also to the 'whole of him', where the content of this elusive phrase is understood both as being related to a set of capabilities and functionings whilst also not exhaustively accounted for in these terms and as having an application even when much in the way of capability is absent or hidden.

All this, admittedly, is vague and speculative.[1] But the question remains as to whether capability theory can supply a complete account of George's status, not only as a loved one, but also as an equal member of our community, and if not, what that implies for the theory, and for George.

5 Concluding remarks

Capability theory provides a fertile resource for anyone writing about disability, and it represents a significant attempt to identify what matters, fundamentally, for an assessment of a person's condition and circumstances. But I have suggested that there are limitations to capability theory as it applies to people with profound disabilities. Freedom is a fundamental human value; but there are other fundamental values which are unrelated to our freedom. The concept of 'capability' cannot be so elastic as to allow us to conclude that all human beings are similarly endowed with capabilities, irrespective of impairment, disability and other facts about us. And I have suggested that there is more to what is valuable about a person, including what they can offer other people, than is likely to be revealed in an audit of their capabilities and functionings.

Points for discussion

- What do you understand by 'human capabilities'?
- What else – if anything – is important about a person's condition besides the capabilities they either possess or might come to acquire?
- What is the place for imagination and hope in thinking about what someone is or might be capable of?
- Are we right to treat people as if they have a capability even if it is likely that this is something that they will never possess?
- Is what a person is entitled to – whether as a citizen or as a pupil – a product of what she is or might be capable of?

Note

1 See McMahan 2002 and 2005 for trenchant criticism.

4

DEPENDENCY AND RECIPROCITY

1 Introduction

Human beings are dependent animals. Fraser and Gordon argue that we should conceive 'dependency' as a normal and often valuable human quality, and they suggest a distinction between 'socially necessary' dependence, 'an inescapable feature of the human condition, experienced particularly intensely in the beginning and end of the life cycle, as well as frequently in between' and 'surplus dependence', rooted in unjust and potentially remediable social institutions (Fraser and Gordon 1977: 629). Whatever we make of this distinction we should acknowledge the numerous basic dependencies that apply to human beings: each of us in infancy is dependent on others for nourishment and nurturing, and all those who fall seriously ill or who become incapacitated are in need of carers to cater to their basic needs. And that is before we consider how social and political developments can undermine personal autonomy, as when unemployment leads to a dependency on the state or other people for even the basic goods that anyone needs to live on.

As a philosopher and mother of a profoundly disabled daughter, Eva Kittay has made a notable contribution to our understanding of the dependency of disabled people, exploring the dimensions of dependence and its place in our understanding of equality, care and justice. She emphasises both the inescapable dependencies rooted in biology, and the extent to which our experience and understanding of dependency is a product of societal attitudes and cultural norms. She also draws attention to the relation between dependency and interconnectedness:

> While conditioned in fundamentally significant ways by cultural considerations, dependency for humans is as unavoidable as birth and death are for all living organisms ... Our dependency, then, is not only an *exceptional* circumstance. To see it as such reflects an outlook that dismisses the

importance of human interconnectedness … I emphasise the most undisputed forms of dependence. Yet attention to just these embraces such a vast proportion of human interactions. My hope is that once we understand the clearest cases of dependency, we will appreciate the full range of human interconnection, and see how all moral and political concepts need to reflect these connections.

(1999: 29–30)

The interconnectedness that Kittay draws attention to will be illustrated throughout the book, including in the discussion of caring for and valuing other people. In this chapter the emphasis is less on the carer and caring relations, and more on dependent people themselves. I offer a series of pen portraits, together with a discussion of their dependencies, relationships and status as citizens, and the conflicting priorities that emerge when the level of dependency leaves a doubt about the possibility of reciprocity and the desirability of pursuing independence. As far as possible, I allow respondents to speak for themselves, both in describing the people they care for and in discussing the issues arising from living with profound dependency.

2 Dimensions of dependency

Rebecca

Rebecca is a profoundly disabled 18-year-old woman, and her principal carers are her parents, Paul and Emma, and Eva, a 24-year-old support worker.

Rebecca has nine diagnoses, the most important of which include Cornelia de Lange syndrome, a developmental disorder characterised by cognitive impairment, skeletal abnormality, distinctive facial features and slow growth before and after birth. She also has a pituitary abnormality, causing multiple endocrine difficulties, including an underactive thyroid and a sub-optimal adrenal response. At the age of 12, Rebecca was diagnosed with bi-polar affective disorder. Rebecca's routine includes ten medications administered at regular intervals throughout each day.

How would her parents describe Rebecca? 'Mischievous; a monkey; a real character. Determined. A bull in a china shop. Rebecca likes people and people tend to like her – when they get to know her. Usually, when the 1:1 support worker at school speaks about Rebecca she laughs. Rebecca is temperamentally easy going – not a difficult person to be with. You do get pleasure from her company when medically things are OK. She can be very single-track minded – wanting the same thing again and again. She can be rough, but never intends harm; she is not malicious, even if she can be a bit clumsy. She's quite hard work because you have to be on the ball all the time.' Paul and Emma attend church, but 'it is difficult to take Rebecca to church – she doesn't fit in with the order of service. Whenever we stand up to sing a hymn Rebecca takes this as a sign that it is time to leave.'

For Eva, Rebecca is, above all, 'mischievous – she's got a fantastic sense of humour. My nickname for her is "Tinker." She's challenging but not aggressive, never violent.' And her parents remark that 'other more able children with learning disabilities take pleasure in her company and in helping her. She is tolerant of other children in her class, including children with more serious behavioural difficulties. She's almost a "peacekeeper".'

Dependency

Rebecca needs 1:1 supervision at all times; she has little sense of danger and cannot talk or use even limited sign language. Although she can walk unassisted she uses a wheelchair when travelling any distance. She needs to go out at least once a day for two hours or more to provide her with stimulation, although it is important to avoid noisy or busy environments which Rebecca may find overwhelming. She has poor fine motor skills and a partially developed chewing mechanism which puts her at risk of choking. She has reduced sensation in her hands and feet, and seeks sensory simulation, particularly vibro-tactile sensations such as those produced by vibrating toothbrushes and massagers. She is subject to extreme mood changes, manifesting themselves in hyperactivity (becoming excitable and sleeping one night in two) or depression – when it can become difficult to rouse her before midday, and when she may then become tearful and subdued.

Emma does not underestimate Rebecca's dependency: 'She is very, totally dependent. With a little bit of help she can have a meal, but you have to supervise very closely. She's a bit rubbish at loading a spoon! She can't prepare food. She can't shop. She can't recognise danger. She needs bathing, dressing, toileting. But she is *not* utterly passive. She is not solely a passive recipient. She can say "No, I don't want to do that" by going on a "sit down strike." She will use whatever means she has got to let you know what she doesn't want. If you get too close you will push you away. She has ways of getting what she wants. What we mean by "total dependency" is, "you can never leave Rebecca alone."'

As the example of Rebecca illustrates, dependency is not equivalent to helplessness; a person may be wholly dependent, in the sense that she cannot be left alone to do anything by herself, whilst nevertheless being able to do many things, and many things by herself, so long as she is supervised. Nor is dependency to be equated with passivity: Rebecca is quite capable of wilfulness, and asserting herself, as her mother is at pains to testify.

For Eva, dependency is 'support with understanding. For example Rebecca needs help to understand what is too hot for her to get close to. She has no sense of danger. She will sit next to a radiator and burn herself if you let her. She would jump into a hot bath. She is dependent on me to cook for her. She knows when she's hungry and she can communicate that to me. When she's had enough she will let you know. But she is *not* totally dependent on me. If she's tired she will take herself to bed. She will stand up, walk to her bedroom, pull back her covers, lie down and go to sleep.' Despite an almost constant need for supervision, Rebecca is capable of acting on her own: she can make decisions, act on them and realise her intentions without any need for assistance.

Rebecca has recently moved into a residential home. Eva remarks that 'Rebecca's new flat is her little world – the carpet, the windows, turning the taps on and off, playing with the safety gate.' For her parents 'her new flat has given her more freedom. If she wants she can wander between rooms, there is more space, she can go and lie down on her bed. We don't any longer have to confine her to one or two rooms.'

Emma and Paul are proud of Rebecca, not only of who she is – 'her mischievousness, her sense of determination, her real sense of humour' – but also of what she can achieve – 'moving away from home, her ability to cope with change, her resilience'. Though constantly dependent on others, Rebecca is adaptable, determined and resilient, and these are characteristics of someone who is acting on and shaping her world, rather than merely passively conforming to it.

At the same time Rebecca remains vulnerable, something Emma is acutely aware of: 'She has relatively little control over what happens to her, at least on a large scale – where she lives, what school she goes to, who her support workers are. For me that is difficult to accept – she is so vulnerable. You worry if you've got it right. You worry for the time when you're not going to be there.' This worry, about how a daughter or son will be looked after in the absence of a mother and father, is among the deepest and most pervasive anxieties that afflict the parents of children with profound disabilities.

Citizenship

What is Rebecca's place in society? 'A lot of people ask after her. And she gets you to think differently – thinking about a person not in terms of how much money they can earn or how much they can contribute to the economy, but what is their ability to be happy, and what is their ability to be nice to people? She will continue in her own little way to learn more and develop further.'

Emma is not inclined to put the limitations in Rebecca's life down to the failings of the society she lives in: 'I don't think her dependency is hugely related to the fact that society hasn't caught up. Her abilities are those of a young toddler and we don't say a toddler's dependencies are down to society. Society may not be ready for "care in the community", not if the person cared for gets too close to them, and starts making unusual or loud noises. We're not sure how much the general public realise that there are people like Rebecca around.'

Citizenship can be conceived as a relationship between citizen and state: the state upholds and provides a set of rights and resources in return for some contribution from the citizenry. One principle that might be invoked here is, 'To each according to their needs; from each according to their ability.' Some people with profound disabilities are not able to fulfil (some part of) a contract such as this; they cannot reciprocate in all the expected ways. But as Emma remarks, this is surely not a reason to cast anyone adrift: 'Rebecca has no means of voicing, let alone enforcing her rights. The crucial thing is that Rebecca should be treated humanely and kindly. Society has to provide for people like Rebecca to be sure they can live in a decent sort of way. She is probably seen as a drain on resources. But society needs to look after her. She's just a human being with a strong personality who should be respected for who she is. Why should she have a bad life just because she has no power to control her own circumstances?'

This is a good question, and it is closely related to some basic questions in political philosophy: whether all but only people who make and produce things are entitled to the fruits of their labour; and whether it is only the people who sign up to the responsibilities and duties included in a 'social contract' – as between themselves and others, or between themselves and the state – who are entitled to the benefits and rewards that any such contractual arrangement brings with it. Many people, besides profoundly disabled people, are neither producers nor active participants in a social contract – not, at least, in any straightforward sense. Emma's question is therefore not a marginal but a central question for contemporary politics, and for any society that seeks to see that justice is done for its many dependent and vulnerable members.

Habibah

Habibah is the 5-year-old daughter of Adiva, who has a second daughter, Basimah, aged 9. Adiva was born in London, her parents in Bangladesh.

Intrauterine growth restriction was diagnosed during Adiva's second pregnancy (poor growth of baby in mother's womb); Habibah now exhibits global developmental delay, and she is visually and aurally impaired. She was diagnosed as having coarctation (narrowing) of the aorta, on which she has since had surgery, and Alagille syndrome, a complex autosomal dominant disorder stemming from defects in the Notch signalling pathway. One of the major features of Alagille syndrome is liver damage caused by abnormalities in the bile ducts. The syndrome is associated with impaired blood flow from the heart into the lungs and it may also affect blood vessels within the brain, the spinal cord and the kidneys. Adiva continues to have rounds of meetings with cardiologists, neurologists and a respiratory team. 'I have to be my own PA [personal assistant] – it's like running a business!'

Under some taxonomies, Habibah would be classified as having 'severe' rather than 'profound' cognitive impairments. This is not to diminish the extent of her impairments, but to emphasise that her capabilities far exceed those of some other people whose learning difficulties are multiple and profound. 'When I look at the smaller picture, within her own community, which includes children who are almost unable to communicate by any means, and who are largely bed-bound, then Habibah is not in that position.'

Habibah is a 'bubbly, happy, playful' girl, a real 'fighter', who is finding her place in the world and enjoying her school. 'I wouldn't change her for the world', Adiva says, 'She means everything to me. My way is, I care for her – I have to care for her. And along with the caring is the loving. If you don't have the love then care is compromised.'

Interaction and reciprocity

Adiva recalls: 'From Basimah I would get a lot of dialogue and feedback; she would make me talk a lot, would want to eat certain things, dress a certain way, would be more vocal. Her presence would be felt more. I'm not saying that Habibah's presence is not felt, but we have got to go close to her in order to engage with her.' In contrast, Habibah uses her senses in ways that Basimah does not. 'Habibah's got that "sixth sense" – I can't really explain it. When she feels the wind in her face – she knows it's a good place, just as she knows if there is something not right. She will feel that. Just as if she has a sixth sense.'

It took a long time for her parents to understand why Habibah's developmental progress was not as rapid as they had expected. Initially it was puzzling as to why Habibah would not look at her parents. 'You give love, you give a smile and you ask, "Why does she not look at my face?"' It was only later, when Habibah's visual and other impairments were better appreciated, that her parents understood why their daughter was not looking at them. 'So now we notice that she is more interested in things that she can hear and play with, like her bangles or her sister's glasses, rather than our faces.' This is an example of what distinguishes life with Habibah: 'We *do* get a lot, but in a different way, like a sixth sense. She won't be direct. It's like, through her senses, through her small movements, we have to mind-read, to understand her.'

It can require a prolonged effort to relate to someone who does not behave and express themselves in ways that we are used to. Reciprocity in relationships need not involve a like-for-like exchange; when it does not, and when one person expends more effort than the other, the exchange may yet be equally rewarding on both sides – both sides 'get a lot', but 'in a different way'.

Dependency, guidance, choice

Whilst encouraging Habibah's development, Adiva emphasises that Habibah remains 'entirely dependent. She needs 24/7 care. On a dependency scale of 1–10 it would be 10+ or 11. Her development is globally delayed. She is not aware of danger, and I have to do everything for her – everything.' What can she do by herself? 'Habibah is not able to groom or clothe herself, or brush her teeth – she needs almost everything done for her. She can sleep, but even then I have to put her to sleep. She can play, but I have to bring the toys to her.' Nor is the level of dependency likely to decline much: 'Such tasks as tying her shoe laces I don't expect she will ever be able to do for herself. Even if she eventually learns to walk, she is likely to tire or trip – so all the time someone must be looking after her.'

'I guide Habibah all the way: she holds her toothbrush and I hold my hand over her hand and I guide her, I see her through every bit of her routine. And that goes on – I will have to guide her all the way through her life. She especially needs guidance if she doesn't enjoy doing something – dressing, clothing, toileting.'

'For Habibah, independence is confined to the little things that she can do and enjoys doing – exploring the floor, bottom crawling, playing with a toy. If she doesn't enjoy doing something, she seems unable to learn – brushing her teeth for example. She probably could have learned it, but she won't if she doesn't enjoy it. Selective play, selective engagement – if she's not happy she will just phase out. But if she likes doing something, it seems that she *can* learn sometimes – I wonder why that is?!'

In a three-year study of learning environments for people with profound and complex learning difficulties, Dee et al. (2002) observed opportunities for learners to make choices about what they did and what was done to them. Features contributing to a choice-enhancing environment included developing learning plans that encourage individuals to do what they can for themselves, and the provision of communication systems that allow individuals to direct what happens to them. Dee emphasises how easy it is to underestimate the obstacles in the way of fostering choice: the time, effort and material resources required to overcome these, and the significance of the small steps taken in an environment that allows for the development of limited independence (ibid.).

Harriet

Harriet is the 22-year-old adopted daughter of Peter and Veronica, who have two other children, Debbie (25) and Sybil (23). Harriet has profound learning, social and behavioural difficulties and disabilities; she is also blind and severely autistic. Otherwise she is 'pretty healthy, and not under any consultant for anything – we have a GP, that's it'. A year ago she moved into a residential care home with seven other profoundly disabled people.

The first words that Peter and Veronica use to describe Harriet are 'complicated' and 'challenging'. 'On her good days Harriet laughs, she sings, she can respond. Music is among the activities that she most enjoys. She loves listening to music, and she loves drums – African drums that she can bash and thump. She has an amazing sense of rhythm. She loves water and swimming and being outside. She likes to be given a packet of straws so that she can chew them and then throw them across the room. But (as with practically everything) we have to initiate.'

Harriet can be hard work. Her behaviour is 'loud, challenging and destructive – of things, towards herself (she will pinch and scratch) and towards other people. She tends to scratch Peter and pull Veronica's hair. When she does it it's never done maliciously or spitefully. It's just "this is what I do." The biggest problem is that Harriet is very loud. She shouts all the time. So we never get (re)invited to anything. There are very few places that Harriet is invited to in the neuro-typical world.'

'Harriet has a good memory for words, but, being echolalic (repeating words spoken by others) she has no idea what they mean, so although she has lots of language she has very little comprehension. Above all she can't communicate what she wants and her biggest struggle is communicating what goes on inside of her. She never says "No". If you say "Do you want to play in a park?" Harriet may say "That is a 'Yes.'" But she may not mean that. She may hate it. When she puts her hand down her clothes and rips her nappies to pieces what she may be trying to say is "I'm bored" or "I want something."'

Veronica remarks that the impact of parenting and living with Harriet has been 'mega huge': 'it has shaped our lives – our other two are almost off our hands but Harriet never will be. Our lives are organised around Harriet.'

Citizenship

For Veronica and Peter any discussion of Harriet's citizenship should emphasise rights and choice: 'We are not all equal, we are all very different. But it's all about *choices*, giving people choices to fulfil their potential. It's about the right to live a life that is fulfilling for her, in whatever way that might be. *It's about the right to be the person you are*. She has the right to be here, with her own voice.'

Both parents remark on difference and citizenship: 'Fundamentally society has a problem with difference. There is something about just accepting that Harriet is Harriet, and that her world is limited and we can come in and come out of it and that is enough.' Any sense of citizenship is 'about the community in which she lives – the group she lives in within her residential community. Harriet's world is small; it's about Harriet. Her citizenship needs to be scaled down to her world.'

If there is a concept of universal citizenship that is to be taken seriously as applying to *all* people, including Harriet, we need to consider what the world looks like to her, and what it demands of her, a perspective that should be represented by guardians in the context of legal and political decision-making. This is necessary if Harriet's 'citizenship' is to be something more than merely an honorific title, and to carry with it practical and binding implications for what we owe her and how she is to be treated.

Dependency and protectiveness

Peter and Veronica concur on the extent of Harriet's dependency: '*Total!* Complete, 100 per cent. Before she moved into her new home we were parents, carers, advocates – we were her eyes, her voice. We struggled with Social Services on this. They regard us as overly protective parents who are unable to let go. They wanted Harriet to be independent; they emphasised her "right to choose". But we said: "OK, but she needs to be guided in everything she does, including her answers." She is dependent on other people for everything, totally. She is still in nappies. She can't wipe her own bottom. Or if she does she might wipe any mess on the floor or throw it on the wall. Social Services are obsessed with choice and independence. The view of Social Services is: "Harriet should be viewed as an independent adult." Social Services want Harriet to have assisted living; they can't see that true independence is out of reach. She can't even make her own food. She can finger feed and use a spoon. But unless it's put in front of her she will starve. She never asks for food. She never says "I'm hungry" or "I'm thirsty." And she has no imaginative play: if it's play with rhythm and tunes then she'll do it. Play is about an adult initiating contact. She plays, but has no idea of what playing is. She doesn't understand "play."'

Peter sums up: 'I don't think Harriet could do any more. I think we've done the best we could.' Veronica adds: 'Harriet's potential is only ever as good as the people who work with her. Her potential is limited by the people around her. It's about the people.'

Peter and Veronica raise a question that applies to all human beings, but it applies in an especially acute form to humans who are profoundly dependent and who are unable to meet by themselves even their most basic needs. That question is: how much importance we should attach to safety, comfort and the avoidance of harm, on the one hand, and, on the other, the capacity to choose, act for oneself and develop one's potential? Parents, carers, teachers and other professionals come face to face with this question all the time, and it requires further discussion.

3 Safeguarding and independence

Frank is the 16-year-old son of Amanda and John. As revealed by Amanda, who also works at the school Frank attends, Frank provides a vivid example of the difficulties of balancing the priorities of safeguarding and independence.

Frank has multiple and profound disabilities, including autistic spectrum disorder, but he does not have multiple and profound *learning* difficulties. Amanda recalls: 'We had no diagnosis until he was four. At that stage it was confirmed that he had severe language and communication delay. But many traits weren't apparent. He wasn't a "textbook case". He is extremely intelligent. He works on the computer and learns himself on the computer. He has a fantastic sense of humour. You can hold a conversation with Frank – on his own terms.'

'When he first went to school, he did not speak, he used to bite, to kick. I never thought he would speak, read, use a computer. But now, on the computer, he wants to know about things that interest him. He loves films, Russell Howard, comedy. He will find out lots about Russell Howard, because he's interested. But things that he is not interested in – showering, getting his own clothes – he doesn't do anything. It's like, "What now?" He just freezes. And I wouldn't trust him with hot water or to regulate the shower. He can toilet himself, but – blimey! – what it took to get him to toilet himself!'

'The thing about Frank is that he has no self-help skills. He has to be adult supervised at all times. He can't shower himself. He will take his own clothes off and then it's, "What do I do now?" He can't take the next step. He is unable to get his clothes out. And he can't be left alone outside. He can't cross the road on his own – he wouldn't even think to look. You tell him, "Look!", but it goes over his head. This part of his brain is so immature. It's the self-help skills that he doesn't have. He can't tie his own shoelaces.'

'If he had been able to look after himself better he would be at college now. Previously he was in a formal class, which follows the national curriculum. Children in the "formal" class can generally speak – they're more on the Asperger's side. They've got learning skills and independence skills. And the kids in this class, they have gone on to college. They walk themselves to college. But my son can't do that; he can't walk by himself. He's what the teachers call "the wavy one in the middle." He's in the middle, between children who can go into a formal class and children who are best suited to a "semi-formal" class, which caters for children who can't be trusted to go independently anywhere.'

What is it like looking after Frank? 'He's a constant worry. He's 6 feet 4 inches. When I go, when my hubby goes, what's going to happen to him? I came to this school because I didn't trust anyone with my son. It's hard to trust people when you have a child who is unable to tell you how their day went. I just didn't trust anybody. You read about it in the paper every day. You convince yourself, you can't trust anybody other than family and people who really know Frank well. So I get no respite, because of his vulnerability.'

And he *is* vulnerable: 'He would open the door to a complete stranger. Once, two years ago, he walked out of the school. He was found at a nearby bus stop. If he had got on the bus ... Oh my God! He doesn't even know what a bus is! He hasn't got a clue. He was only round the corner. He didn't think: "I can just walk back to the school." So I've now given him an engraved bracelet with my name and address.'

'The school was saying to me "Give him independence. Give him independence", but after that incident, with the bus stop, the school knows better. Even the school was shocked that he could do that. That was scary. He doesn't think. He just goes.'

The difficulties of encouraging children to do more than they might otherwise will be familiar to all parents, as they are to Elisabeth Peters, Head of Christ Church School. She recalls one child, Geeta, who was two or three at the time of the episode, and who used to cry all day when at nursery school. Elisabeth supposed that this was because she had been taken out of the physical space that she knew, which was being 'carried' by her mother. Elisabeth wanted to encourage Geeta to feel comfortable without being held all the time, although she was also concerned to 'do all the "school" things – providing physiotherapy, a supportive chair and so on'. However: 'What Geeta wanted more than anything else was *to be held by her mother.*' Elisabeth oversaw an uneasy compromise, when some of the 'naughty' staff carried Geeta about for some of the time. She concedes that these staff were probably right, and that what the school should have done is to move more slowly.

Marjorie Clarke, Head of St Peter's School, explains that the aims in her school are sensitive to children's stages of development: 'For some of our children the aim is independence – so that the children are equipped to do as much as they can for themselves. Not enough attention is given to how support might be reduced so as to reduce learned helplessness. Suppose someone prefers to be passive only because that is what they are used to? Take an example of one of my young boys. He had a tracheostomy when very young, and an oxygen canister, to counter any risk to his swallowing. Consequently he needed an adult with him at all times and 1:1 support. At the age of six the tracheostomy was removed and his level of 1:1 support was reduced. At first he couldn't cope – his behaviour became very difficult – and as a result the 1:1 support was increased in order to help him to cope better with the transition. Now we have found his behaviour has improved considerably: he is walking independently and cycling independently (with an adapted bicycle). This shows that any judgement about how far a child needs to be supported, and how far he can and should be encouraged to become more independent, is not always an easy one – it's easy to underestimate.'

Marjorie has one especially vivid anecdote in which she took a risk by encouraging children to show evidence of independence in the presence of an Ofsted inspector. 'With the inspector present we once observed a Key Stage 1 class with a teacher who was encouraging the children to explore fruit and vegetables. Initially each child had 1:1 support from a teaching assistant who was encouraging the children to touch, smell and look at what was in front of them. The teacher had a gong and announced that, when he banged the gong the adults were all to stop what they were doing. With the banging of the gong all the adults froze – we were anxious about what was about to happen. And for all of two or three minutes – an eternity during an inspection! – none of the children moved. I noticed that the inspector had begun to write, "A brave attempt to encourage independent activity but regrettably it failed … " But just as he was completing the sentence the children began to move and then to start exploring the fruit and vegetables in front of them! The exercise was a success and the Inspector had to cross out what he had written. It shows that sometimes children can be encouraged to do rather more than what might have been expected.'

The dilemmas and risks described here are sometimes as difficult as they are because they involve a conflict between basic priorities: on the one hand, the importance of protecting humans from danger, and ensuring that they are safe and comfortable; on the other, the importance of encouraging them to grow and to flourish, so that they can live life to their full potential. A conservatively risk-averse policy may leave some children living well within themselves; expectations often adapt to existing constraints so as to lead to an excessively cautious view about prospects for change in the future. But equally, a policy that values autonomy and independence before all else runs the risk of leaving children exposed to harm and emotional disturbance, struggling to manage the demands that go along with making choices and having to live with the consequences.

Perhaps the most acute dilemmas arise for children with severely life-limiting conditions who experience a lot of pain and distress. For their parents the first priority is to avoid suffering and maintain a minimum level of comfort, and any attempt to encourage independence will be thought of as a secondary concern, or, at the very least, as something that should not pose any risk to the child's sense of security and wellbeing. There are other examples, too: children whose capacity for living an independent life may be increased, but only following an immense effort, leading to improvements that are slight or temporary, and which may themselves cause the children and their carers more distress and discomfort than they would want to live with.

Almost everyone featured in this book would stand four square behind autonomy and independence as guiding values in their lives as parents, carers and teachers. For schools in particular these values could almost be said to constitute their *raison d'etre*, and nothing written here should be read as calling that into question. At the same time there remain unavoidably hard questions, arising from the simple fact that it is not always obvious how we should weigh the fundamental goods of being comfortable, and free of pain and distress, alongside the opportunity to live life to one's full potential.

4 Reciprocity

Smith has written that the 'degree to which a relationship is dependent ... is usually in inverse proportion to the level of reciprocity that is perceived to exist within that relationship' (2001: 579–580). I will suggest that this is a mistake; it is easy to underestimate the extent of reciprocity, and this perhaps explains a tendency to exaggerate the varying levels of dependency between people. Kittay understands this better than most. She does not underestimate the dependency of her daughter, who has profound cognitive impairments, cerebral palsy and seizure disorders, but the dependency is not only her daughter's: 'I depend on her as well ... Others could take care of her and even love her – in fact I must think that she will continue to thrive with or without me. But without her, I would wither' (2001: 576).

Kittay suggests that 'dependency', in the sense that someone is unable to reciprocate in any way at all, is rare and likely to apply only to those persons who are comatose or unconscious (2001). Certainly it does not apply to all profoundly disabled persons simply in virtue of their disabilities and dependencies; profound dependency is often compatible with fulfilling and reciprocal relationships, although, as we will see shortly, there are people whose capacity for reciprocity is slight.

Parenting and reciprocity

Profound dependency has a lifelong impact on relationships between parents and children, as with Peter, Veronica and Harriet. What is a 'relationship' for Harriet? According to Veronica it's '"Meeting my needs, when I want you to do it." She has people in her life, who are important to her, but I'm not convinced she *understands* love and that sort of thing. She knows Peter as "dad" and me as "mum" but I don't know what this means to her. I know she enjoys our company sometimes, but it's about what she gets out of it – it's not a two-way process.' Peter agrees: 'It's one way; you give, give, give and don't expect anything back. But just occasionally you do get something back.' For Veronica, as her mother, 'this is the hardest challenge. I love my daughter ... but it's hard to keep on loving whilst knowing that you're not going to get anything back. What is Harriet's conception of what it means to be loved or to love? It's about her basic needs, and as long as her basic needs are met, that's enough for her.'

Whilst Rebecca's disabilities place limits on communication with her parents, her mother, Emma, never doubts that her daughter loves her: 'I never really struggled with the concept that she loved me in her way. I didn't ever feel that there wasn't some kind of emotional bond there.' Eva, Rebecca's support worker, is adamant: 'People may think that she doesn't show love; she *does* show love. She can't verbalise it. She will grab your hand and sit there and hold your hand. Sometimes it's for you if you've had a bad day. I really think she can love – seeing her interact with her parents and support workers. Not with words or the way we – you and me – do it. She can't say it. She can't use words, but she can understand.'

Paul and Emma emphasise that 'communication for Rebecca is not just a way of saying that she wants something – it can be a way of *being* with someone. Sometimes she will sit with you, and pat or stroke your hands – that's a sign that she's happy to be with you. This is a "being with" communication – there is, for Rebecca, just the pleasure of being with you.' Emma remarks that 'she might grab my hand, go and lie in bed, and that's a signal that she wants me to follow her and sing to her. We're not doing much – we're just being together.'

For Eva the reward is great: 'I get more out of spending time with Rebecca than some of my friends. Making her smile when she's sad. Every day is different. She's so much more than a "support plan." The joy of the little things is the most amazing thing about her. Rebecca will see the joy in a leaf. She likes the leaf, picks it up and plays with it. It's the little things. Textures. She loves textures. She likes the feel of covers, she touches them, licks them as well. Watching her really does give you joy, because she can find joy in everything.'

Even some of the most profoundly dependent children can give back to their carers more than the children themselves will have any idea of. I recounted previously how much Pamela needs and takes from George, her 6-year-old profoundly disabled son who is utterly dependent on her: 'He's not just a child who sits in a wheelchair: he's given me *so much*. Before George was born, I wouldn't be here in the room talking to you. I wouldn't speak to anyone. I was *very* shy. I've had to become his voice, I've had to fight for things. You have to ask, and asking for anything is a big thing to do when you've never done it before. Also, I've learned to drive. And I've met some amazing people – some amazing mums. He's given me *masses*. I owe him everything.'

It isn't only Pamela whose life George has changed, but others in the family: 'Having George brought me and [her partner] Nick closer together as a team' and Susan, 20, the youngest of three daughters 'loves George to bits – and being his sister is why she's studying child care and education'.

Lack of reciprocity

Someone may be almost totally dependent on others, and still give back as much, or almost as much, as she receives. But is this true for all children? I have described Sam elsewhere, the boy of whom his teacher Daniel remarked, 'Frankly there is nothing going on and there never will be', but who, amazingly, one day responded to the sound of a bell, a 'miracle' that has never been repeated. It is not easy for a teacher, or anyone, to care for a child who is as unresponsive as Sam, who will often sleep through much of the day, and appears not to respond to anything other than a favourite food. What motivates Daniel? 'Outside of work I would think of Sam as "just there." But I am emotionally involved with Sam. I want him to be as comfortable as possible. He is a boy in my class. I care for his wellbeing. He probably won't have a long life. I want him to enjoy his life as much as he can. And particularly him more than the others – because Sam is so passive. Things are done to Sam, he doesn't do anything for himself. If you left Sam on the floor and came back the next day he would still be in the same position. He can't roll. Yet at some deeper level there may be a connection with Sam – even though he can't express anything. Sam is another human being. I can help him, and I do feel that I have a connection because in many respects he is like me. And I believe it's important for me to do the best I can for him – because I can.'

Daniel does not pretend that it's easy. He acknowledges that he will gravitate towards children with higher-level abilities because he knows that he can expect a response from them. Some of these children might reach out to hold his hands, unlike Sam, who has neither the ability nor the instinct to do this. 'He might be loved, but in the context I know him I genuinely don't think that he has any awareness of being loved. Sometimes I ask, "What's the point?" I know it's just not going to happen. Maybe somebody more skilled than me would elicit more from Sam, but I can't.'

Nadifa is a 5-year-old Somalian girl, who in Daniel's opinion is the lowest functioning child at St Peter's School. Her disabilities are in large part a product of medical negligence when she was a baby. She is small, well dressed and always has braids in her hair. Daniel has worked with her for three months. She has severe global developmental delay, scoliosis and cerebral palsy. She will vocalise when having a seizure, but not otherwise, not even when she is cold or hungry, or when she has soiled herself. She can move her eyes and has some limited movement in her arms. But as Daniel puts it 'the bottom line is that she can do nothing for herself'. Unless he is pro-active there is nothing she would do. 'Even if I were to put her hand in cold water I doubt very much that she would withdraw it. Basically, if I do nothing, she will do nothing.' How does one care for a human being who appears to do so little and give very little back? 'I'm not overly connected emotionally. Nadifa doesn't give a lot. She just exists. She's there physically, but that's really it. But another part of me feels that she's hard done by as a result of other people's incompetence. She will never be better physically and mentally but she could perhaps be more comfortable. I care for her wellbeing and want her to achieve as much as she can. She is after all a pupil in my class.'

Does Daniel have any kind of relationship with Nadifa? 'Because I don't get anything back from Nadifa it's difficult to foster a relationship with her. Out of all the pupils in the class I have less of a relationship with her than others. It is not a two-way thing. It's very much "me to her." Maybe "all me to her." Perhaps there is some potential for her to give something, but it wouldn't matter to me if there was no prospect of getting anything back. Because of the nature of Nadifa's difficulties, I can't expect much in the way of a two-way relationship.'

Dependency is related to reciprocity, but not in any simple way, and not in the way that Smith suggests. A child may be both wholly dependent on her parents, and yet reciprocate in ways that are found to be as deep and rewarding as anything the parents themselves offer. But there are some cases – very few – in which a state of total dependency is accompanied by an almost complete incapacity for reciprocity. This prompts reflection on the meaning and value of relationships, and of caring relations generally. Daniel's testimony is arresting: if one goes on receiving nothing back, one may finally come to ask, 'What's the point?' But yet, when speaking of Sam, Daniel is also moved to say that it is important to do his best for him – 'because he is a human being, like me, and because I can'.

5 Concluding remarks

Each human being is extensively dependent on other people; an obvious, basic truth that does not always get the attention it deserves. The fact and implications of dependency, and our interconnectedness, can be lost sight of, or obscured, by an outlook characterised by an emphasis on individual autonomy and personal independence.

The fact of universal dependency should be seen alongside another basic truth: that the dependencies of some people are much greater than those of others, and to the point that their capacity for autonomy and independence is significantly curtailed. In a few cases this capacity is vanishingly small, and this raises hard questions in practice and theory about how it is best to regard people such as Sam and Nadifa.

'Dependency' is not a simple idea; dependency in one respect may go along with interdependence or independence in others. Even profound dependency allows for reciprocity in personal relationships that less dependent members find inexhaustibly valuable and fulfilling. Perhaps this explains why an able bodied and independent parent should consider herself (almost) as dependent on a profoundly disabled child as her child is dependent on her. Recall Kittay's remark about her daughter: 'I depend on her as well … without her, I would wither' (2001: 576).

Points for discussion

- Is anyone totally dependent on other people?
- There is no such thing as 'total independence': discuss.
- What is the connection between dependency and reciprocity?
- To what extent can we reconcile the aims of protecting profoundly disabled people from harm and encouraging their independence?
- At what point should we say that someone's safety and wellbeing comes before any attempt to encourage their capacity for autonomy and independence?

5

VALUING PROFOUNDLY DISABLED PEOPLE

In practice

1 Introduction

In Chapter 6 we will look at the value and moral status of profoundly disabled human beings as writers and theoreticians see these things. Here I turn to what people say about the value of the human beings they themselves care for, teach and parent; and not only to what they say but also to what they are prepared to do on behalf of their loved ones and the children they look after.

In section 2 parents speak about their love for their children, and I look at how love can reveal what is most precious in a human being. In section 3 I explore the difficulties that arise when love and care are not always returned or recognised, but consider, also, how much profoundly disabled children bring to people's lives, whether or not love is reciprocated in kind. Faith, religious or otherwise, lies at the centre of the lives of many parents and teachers, as illustrated in section 4, whilst in section 5 I acknowledge that love and the value of human life are difficult subjects to find adequate words for.

2 Love

Words, feelings, actions

I could have filled a book with the testimony of parents speaking of how much they love their children. Krystyna, first introduced in Chapter 2, is the 28-year-old Polish mother of James, who is 5: 'James is a special boy – for me, his father, my parents, my family. He's like … our angel. He's my life, my angel, he's everything to me, I'd do anything for him, I'd die for him. I don't know how I would feel if I had another child, but I think James would be *more* special – because he needs me, he needs love.'

Vivienne might have said the same. She is the 48-year-old mother of Stephen, a profoundly disabled boy of 8. She also has three daughters, Katie, 28, Jane, 26 and

Susan, 20. 'I love all my children the same. He's my only boy. He has a different kind of love.' 'Different' – does Vivienne love Stephen any less than her daughters? 'No, no, no … . *More*, I reckon. I wouldn't change him for the world.' Stephen has a level of functioning that is limited, even by comparison with other profoundly disabled children. He cannot communicate with language and Vivienne often has to guess at how best to interpret any vocalisation, even when this relates to his basic needs. Yet her love for him is undiminished. She loves him, perhaps, in spite of, or partly because of the profoundly disabled boy that he is; or perhaps his disabilities are largely irrelevant to any explanation of what she feels for Stephen. How can we account for this? We might say, with Gaita, that 'we love what is precious to us, and things are precious to us because we love them' (2004: 122). What he is implying is that human beings are valuable not only in virtue of their intrinsic characteristics but also just because we love them; our love is a source of value in itself, and not just a response to what is valuable. Frankfurt says something similar:

> There are things that become important to us, or that become more important to us than they would otherwise be, just by virtue of the fact that we care about them … It is not necessarily as a *result* of recognising their value and of being captivated by it that we love things. Rather, what we love necessarily *acquires* value for us *because* we love it.
>
> *(2004: 21; 38–39)*

Love is itself a source of the value we might find in anyone, irrespective of their disabilities. The maternal love of Vivienne and Krystyna is no less because their children are able to do less than other children, and, in their eyes the value of their children is in no way diminished because their capacities are more limited than those of most other people.

Charlotte Hallam would say something similar. She is the single mother of two children – Chris, aged 19, who is profoundly disabled, and Kelly, her healthy 14-year-old daughter. Chris has Ring Chromosome 22: he is unable to communicate using language, his capacity for vocalisation is severely limited, he is unable to nod in order to affirm or deny what is asked, although he can, with an effort, blink to indicate 'yes' or 'no'; he is deaf and doubly incontinent; and his behaviour is 'complex' – he frequently harms himself, and, in consequence, he sleeps in a locked and padded bedroom. But this in no way detracts from what Charlotte feels: 'I love Chris to bits! I love Chris as much as I do Kelly. Chris didn't ask for any of this to happen to him. I don't see why he should have any less than Kelly. I don't see why he should be worth any less.'

Without being prompted Charlotte mulls over who she would choose to save if she couldn't save both of her children: 'If I had to save Kelly or Chris's life – obviously I would save Kelly. Because she is able to do a lot more in her life than Chris will ever be able to do.'

Philosophers invite reflection on situations like this, asking us, for example, how we should decide on whom to put in a lifeboat which isn't large enough for everyone.

We are encouraged to think about who matters most if we really had to make a choice. (Some people consider this exercise as objectionable, and refuse to make a choice.) Charlotte tells us that she would choose Kelly over Chris. Does this suggest that, when push comes to shove, Charlotte values Kelly more than Chris? It is hard to tell, particularly when we learn of the lengths to which Charlotte went to keep Chris alive: 'I went through an awful lot for Chris at the beginning. He has a lot of medical problems. We shouldn't have kept him this long. When I first had him I was told that he wasn't going to survive, that "he was running a marathon and he'd never reach the finishing line." Well, we were in the hospital for a year and a half – they only let us out on day release! I nearly lost him on several occasions. It was very tough.'

Imagining what she would do if she had to choose, Charlotte would save Kelly before Chris. But Charlotte chose to stay in hospital for 18 months rather than give him up as lost. She would not let him go. What people say, and what is revealed by their actions about what they think, and what they are prepared to do, is not always the same. It can be important to think carefully about what it is right to do in circumstances we are fortunately not actually in. But equally it can be important to examine our actions when forced to act and not only to think about some imaginary scenario. Charlotte's testimony calls to mind the maxim, 'actions speak louder than words'; at any rate, what is either said or done in the name of love may not make for an altogether clear and coherent picture, and parents may not themselves understand why and how much they love and value their children, even when they manifestly 'love them to bits'.

What love reveals

Love is not only a *source* of value; it may also *reveal* what is precious in a loved one. And what is precious is not simply a capacity we hadn't seen before; it is the human being as a whole, someone who previously we may have written off as inert and devoid of personality, but whose individuality is made manifest in the presence of people who love him and treat him with respect and tenderness.

Gaita tells a story about how in the 1960s he had worked in a psychiatric hospital where some patients had been kept for over 30 years. The hospital reminded Gaita of a zoo:

> When patients soiled themselves, as some did often, they were ordered to undress and to step under a shower. The distance of a mop handle from them, we then mopped them down as zoo-keepers wash down elephants.
>
> *(2000: 17)*

The patients were judged to be incurable and they looked to have lost everything that might give meaning to their lives: no self-respect, no visitors and often treated brutishly by the psychiatrists and nurses. A few of the psychiatrists, however, were seen to work hard to improve the conditions of patients, and they even spoke of their 'inalienable dignity':

One day a nun came to the ward. In her middle years, only her vivacity made an impression on me until she talked to the patients. Then everything in her demeanour towards them—the way she spoke to them, her facial expressions, the inflexions of her body—contrasted with and showed up the behaviour of those noble psychiatrists. She showed that they were, despite their best efforts, condescending, as I too had been. She thereby revealed that even such patients were, as the psychiatrists and I had sincerely and generously professed, the equals of those who wanted to help them; but she also revealed that in our hearts we did not believe this.[1]

(Ibid.: 18–19)

This suggests that the love of one human being for another can disclose the value and preciousness of the beloved or cared for. Speaking of the nun, Gaita writes:

Seeing her ... I felt irresistibly that her behaviour was directly shaped by the reality which it revealed. I wondered at her, but not at anything about her except that her behaviour should have, so wondrously, this power of revelation ... her behaviour was striking not for the virtues it expressed, or even for the good it achieved, but for its power to reveal the full humanity of those whose affliction had made their humanity invisible. Love is the name we give to such behaviour.

(Ibid.: 19–20)

Listening to parents talk about their children, watching them together at play, observing a skilled teacher hold a trembling child, comfort him with infinite tenderness after a seizure, or tease him so as bring a twinkle to his eye; seeing all this has something of the effect that the nun had on Gaita. Love reveals what is most precious about those children who have no words to make any claim on the world, to stand up for their rights, to speak out when they are in pain or even to ask for anyone's love. Love, we might say, is what makes their humanity visible (ibid.).

   The revelatory aspect of loving care was shown to me during a visit to the Litster School, to observe a class of eight children aged between 9 and 10, along with their six teachers and teaching assistants. One of the least responsive children was Mahmoud, a 9-year-old boy who seemed barely awake, slumped in his chair, dribbling, motionless, unseeing eyes more often closed than open. The teaching assistant working with Mahmoud – Kelly – was a large, burly, tattooed woman in her thirties, and someone you wouldn't want to get on the wrong side of. Mahmoud appeared for all the world as if he was entirely oblivious to everything around him. There was very little sign of life. He began to cough violently and Kelly was concerned that he might start to fit. She moved with the grace of a ballet dancer and gently wrapped her huge arms round Mahmoud, patting his chest and back, speaking softly in a re-assuring tone. He was calmed and the anxiety dissipated. He reached out to hold her hand, with wide awake eyes, and she held his hand in the manner of someone supremely assured in knowing how to treat a child who is frightened and helpless, and to hold him so that he feels safe and loved. This episode was over in a minute and in its way was entirely unexceptional: this sort of thing happens day in day out. But the incident revealed Kelly as an accomplished and sensitive carer, and Mahmoud as a vulnerable young child in immediate need of expert care, and who, having received it, no longer appeared as an inert lump in a wheelchair, but as a wide-awake boy doing something quintessentially human – placing his hand in the hand of another. It was a sign of their humanity.

3 Contribution and human worth

Lack of reciprocity

Not all children are able to contribute much to a human relationship. I have described Nadifa and her teacher Daniel in Chapter 4. Nadifa is a 5-year-old Somalian girl who is operating at the lowest level of development that her school is able to accommodate. There is almost nothing she can do for herself, and she will do nothing if nothing is done for her. When I press Daniel on whether Nadifa is in *any* kind of relationship with him, he pauses a while before answering 'Categorically – no.' Yet he obviously cares for her and values her even in the absence of reciprocity: 'Nadifa can't do many things but that doesn't take away from her worth. She matters, just as much as any other child matters in the school. She might be left on the periphery, because she may not get involved, but she matters to me as much. I care for her as much. Despite her limitations she is an equal member of society. To me she is, even if most others would consider her as pretty worthless.'

In Daniel's eyes Nadifa is our equal, even though, by comparison with most people with profound disabilities, there are many things that she is unable to do. I have written 'even though', but Daniel might have written, 'just because': 'In terms of the right to be an equal member of society then, despite her limitations she is very much a human being with human needs – more so because she doesn't have cognitive abilities. She can't do things for herself so she should be especially cared for – because she is almost helpless.'

When a colleague of Daniel's was asked who he would miss more if Nadifa and his pet dog were to die, the colleague replied that it would be his pet dog. Daniel was shocked. He has a cat, which he loves, but he would miss Nadifa more, not least because Nadifa is someone he can *identify* with: 'A cat is a cat. Nadifa is another human being. I have a connection with her because in some respects she is like me. She looks like me. She's a human being. I'm sure she has a soul. I believe it's important for me to do the best I can for her – because I can.'

It is not so much Nadifa's distinguishing characteristics to which Daniel is appealing, although it is significant that she is a human being who also looks like him; it is, above all, the fact that he can identify with Nadifa much more than he can identify with his cat or with some other non-human animal. Nadifa is our 'fellow creature' – someone who belongs to the same species as the rest of us. And the implication of Daniel's words is that he is right to be more concerned about a human being than he is about a cat just because this human being – Nadifa – is someone we can recognise as being one of us. This takes us onto the question of whether species membership is related to our value as human beings, a question we will return to in the next chapter.

'He gave so much'

The lives of profoundly disabled people encourage us to think generously about what someone is able to offer. Rameen Gurmani is a British Pakistani professional mother, married to Tariq, and they have two children, Aisha, their 4-year-old daughter, and Usama, their 6-year-old son who was born with microcephaly and severe learning difficulties. Rameen acknowledges that Usama has made her 'more accepting of people who are different', and she can see how much her life is enriched by what Usama has taught her: 'It's definitely made me a better person. I am definitely more patient, more accepting, more tolerant. My brother says "You're a changed person!"' Rameen has grown to more and more appreciate Usama, and what he can do, and to understand what other people are going through: 'I'm more appreciative of what other people go through. I understand that everything Usama does is a gift. I am more considerate, and I also appreciate how much more Usama can do than other children whose difficulties are more profound. I am grateful for even the little things – his learning to say a few words, or learning to walk. These are little miracles! And he has made us stronger than we were – we've been able to deal with a lot more than we ever thought we could.'

Charlotte Hallam is candid about how Chris has changed her life: 'Before I had Chris I was a very selfish person. I only had me to think about. Chris brought me down to earth. I think that, having Chris, I am a better person. He made me grow up. Now, I make a hell of lot of sacrifices. I have to think a lot before I do anything. I have moments when I think "How different life would be if I hadn't had Chris!", but, basically, I have kind of accepted.'

I introduced Adwoa Nyalemegbe and her son Kwame in Chapter 2. Kwame died in 2005, two weeks before his sixteenth birthday. Adwoa also lost her other two children, one following a premature birth, the other following complications arising from profound disabilities. Having lost all of her children, the words that follow, about what Kwame gave to her life and to those who knew him, are all the more arresting: 'He was *not* less than others. One of his siblings said: "He's such a character!" They adored him. He brought such joy to us. He bought little things that we would never have known of if it wasn't for Kwame. He was so full of joy – it's indescribable. He was a great member of the family, and we all adored him. Our life was so *empty* when he passed away. We all felt less without him.'

People are valued for who they are, and also for what they give to us, what they mean to us, whether the joy they bring into the world or the wretched emptiness they leave behind when they are no longer here. They also teach us about ourselves, as Kwame taught Adwoa: 'Kwame taught me patience and humility. Before, I was bit like a perfectionist. I didn't have any patience. I had to learn patience. Kwame had to be fed and toileted and this all took a long time. I needed patience for that. He also taught me humility: he made me look at things differently in life. And when we lost his sister we got more support from Kwame than from his father. When he came back from school, during the hard days following her death, he would come home, and put a smile on his face, as if to say, "Mummy, let's get on with it."'

Adwoa recalls how Kwame supported her, constantly, through all their ups and downs, including during their innumerable visits to hospitals, and especially during the last months of his life, when it proved impossible to eliminate a constant chest infection. 'During one appointment a consultant had said, in the presence of Kwame, that his swallowing was not functioning as it ought to, that this was a serious and worrying symptom, and that we would need to return for a further consultation in the near future. I was *so* upset and tearful. From the expression on his face it was obvious that Kwame was a bit mad with the doctor for giving me such news. The doctor could see this and he had to offer some reassurance and explain what was going on. He had to apologise for upsetting mummy! So we had our lows, our endless hospital visits hearing things we didn't want to hear, and yet, in spite of all that, Kwame gave me such joy and support, and we just carried on. Because he was also quick to tell you, "Please mummy, cheer up!", just as he would often use his little book to say to me, "Don't cry anymore!"'

Adwoa conveys an unforgettable sense of the preciousness of Kwame and his legacy: 'When I think of him now what comes to mind is *joy*. I think he had a happy life – a good, short life. He gave so much love and joy – you couldn't help but give this back in return.' At the end of our interview Adwoa looked me straight in the eye: 'The simple thing to say is this. I personally believe that it was an *honour* for me to be his mother. I did his journey with him and it was an honour. I don't even think that I deserved this great joy. And until I go to my grave I will always remember my son as a great chapter in my life. He was amazing; the places he took me; the times we had together. In my 53 years I've done many things, but nothing that was as profound and valuable to me as the journey I made with my son.'

Adwoa was silent for a moment and then wished aloud that Kwame would himself have been able to say 'I've had a great time!' But she recalled his cheekiness: 'He would probably have said – "No, I didn't!" just to tease mummy, and then turn around and say, "Yes, I did!"'

Not every parent could say the same as Adwoa, who is herself, like her son, an exceptionally strong and positive person. But those children who are remembered for the love and joy they gave to others have made a lasting contribution, and it is exactly this kind of contribution that is repeatedly mentioned, not only by doting parents, but also by teachers when recalling some of the most profoundly disabled children in their schools. Whilst there are contributions more elaborate and enduring, to be known for having brought a smile to people's faces is a real and lasting legacy nevertheless.

4 Faith

Faith, of one kind or another, is omnipresent in the lives of many carers. Not uncommonly faith goes along with religious belief. Mary Rogers has two children, one of whom, Graham, is profoundly disabled. Mary is Catholic: 'I think that God sent Graham to me because I can deal with it. We're Catholic. Graham comes to church with me. It's amazing. He comes to church now. I could *never* have taken him before.' Mary is fiercely protective towards her son. 'Graham deserves as much as any child. And that's why I am going to make sure that he gets it. He deserves happiness, respect, confidence. He deserves as much as any adult – *of course he does*. In my eyes he is no different to any able child, in what he deserves.'

Is there anything that Mary would change? 'If someone were to say, "Can I take the autism away?" I would say, "Yes, of course." But if I were able to live forever I'd keep him as he is. I wouldn't change a thing. He's a gift. But because I'm not here forever – that's the only reason I'd change him. Because of his future.'

If only Mary could remain with Graham throughout his life there is nothing about him that she would change: Graham is a gift, not to be tampered with even if that would make for an easier life.

Gabrielle Thibault is the single mother of three children, and her youngest, Odette, aged 5, has profound learning difficulties. Her faith is sustaining, and encourages acceptance of how life has turned out: 'I'm Christian. I pray every day, every weekday morning before the day starts. But not always at weekends – being a single mother I need rest! It gives me peace to read the Bible. God knows what he is doing. It is for me and my family to draw close to God. We don't expect no pain, no hurt, no sickness. We don't expect peace. We just learn to accept what comes our way.'

Some parents not only accept how things are but also believe that this is how things were meant to be. This is Krystyna's view, whose son James she has described as 'my life, my angel'. Like Mary, Krystyna is formidably strong. She has her pride too; she doesn't ask for sympathy. Krystyna believes that James was 'meant to be born like this', since 'God chooses the parents who can cope': 'Friends often say, "I couldn't cope with this. You are very strong; that's why God gave this to you. I just couldn't cope." My Christian faith is very important to me. I go to church. I ask Saint Maria to help me, or, not help *me*, but, help my boy. I can do it, but I want my boy to enjoy a little bit of his life. It's not his fault that he was born like this. Sometimes, I think, "Is it my fault that he's born like this?" But my faith is strong. I will support him, help him.'

Phillippa Cauldwell, a teacher at Mayfield School, and first introduced in Chapter 2, observes that faith has taught her that 'life is not all about me – I need to ask "what can I give?" There must be some give and take.' For Phillippa the life of each child at Mayfield is a miracle: 'A human life is a human life. I see conception as a miracle. A life is a precious thing. There is an element in all these children of, "There but for the grace of God go I." Yes, we all have different capacities, but I believe that each person has their place, no matter what capacities they have –

whether they have a PhD or are just breathing. Each individual life, whether the Queen's or one of my little P1 children,[2] is equally precious. All the children are equally precious no matter what they can do.'

Rowan Williams, the former Archbishop of Canterbury, offers some reflections that would appeal to people of many faiths, and of none.[3] For Williams, we can see a person as someone who is the focus for a network of relationships, as being at the centre of this world, even if the 'signals' of their presence and contribution are attenuated. Sometimes the signals are few and far between but at the same time: 'I'm struck by parents who talk to their children whilst clearly not expecting a response. Yet their expectation is not entirely fictive; they are seeking to include their children not as a conversational partner but as part of an affectionate relationship.'

There is an element of 'imaginative charity' at work here, where we imagine that someone is worthy of our time and affection. And whilst what we imagine may extend beyond the facts, this is not to say that it has *no* basis in fact. Moreover, the facts may take us by surprise: 'I recently visited severely disabled and very poor children in the West Bank. People who work in this field are regularly astonished. When I touch a deaf and blind child, his hand reached out to mine. When I blessed a child, he raised his hands above his hands and clapped.'

Williams regards it as an especially important act of imaginative charity that we should be able to imagine someone '*as in some sense capable of love*'. And this is a thought that anyone, with or without religious belief, might have. But Williams also offers a reflection on being the object of love: 'Every human individual is the object of the same kind of unconditional affirming love as you and I are. The love of God is not conditional on achievement; each person is one of innumerable created reflections of the divine beauty.'

This is the unconditional affirmation we find in Mary, Gabrielle, Krystyna and Phillippa; but it is also present in people who may not have religious belief. Sheila Evans, Deputy Head at Mayfield School, has worked with a few children whose lives are curtailed, and whose quality of life is such that, when they pass away, there is among the grief and sorrow a sense of blessed relief. Yet she has no doubt that these children have a precious connection with their teachers and carers. How does she know? 'I don't know. A lot of what we do is an act of faith.' She allows that there is always a risk of 'reading into' someone's behaviour more than their behaviour warrants: 'Teachers can read stuff into behaviour that isn't there – we need to be robust in analysing what an event or situation demonstrates.' But the really important point is this: 'Once we strip away all the "reading into stuff" we've never had a child who can't make a connection, given the right support. And this is the most fundamental human right – to have someone you can have a relationship with. This is just inherently and fundamentally valuable.'

And this applies especially to some of the children Sheila works with, whose short lives include a lot of pain. Wouldn't it be better to let some of these children go? 'I've known a lot of very sick children and I've known only two of whom I would say "the time is right for them to pass away." But I've never known a child of whom I would say "It would have been better if they had never lived." There is always something they have found, including connections with loved ones, that is enjoyable and meaningful to them. Of course, for some families life can become almost intolerable. Yet even then someone will call the doctor, the hospital – they want their child's life saved, and they are absolutely distraught when they go.'

There is in fact no one that Sheila is prepared to give up on: 'I put myself in their position. My own self has a need to be heard, listened to and understood. I wouldn't want someone to give up on me, just because it is hard. So why would I give up on somebody else?'

This is one way of expressing the Golden Rule, 'Do unto others as you would have them do to you', a maxim invoking reciprocity between people, and expressed in many of the world's religions and in humanistic codes of ethics. Yet Sheila also recognises that there can come a time when the prospect of an end to constant suffering is not unwelcome: 'I don't think I have a right to tell you what your quality of life is and should be. But when I saw one of my pupils struggling to breathe, day after day after day, the constant suctioning, his repeated chest infections, one thing after another, and the distress that this caused him, I had a sense of relief when, finally, after his passing, that was finished and he didn't have to suffer any more.'

Even in such a case as this, when it is a great relief that someone should suffer no more, when a child's life was brief and burdened, there may be a legacy that not everyone can claim for themselves. Sheila once said to a father: 'Your son has made a lot of people happy because he lived. Not all healthy people can say that.'

Faith in the children they work with is, indeed, pervasive among people working in special schools: 'faith' not in any (obvious) religious sense but in the sense of believing in the children, believing that they matter as much as anyone else, that they can and will do more and better – that they will get there, wherever 'there' is. Muriel Alexander is Head of Alfred Marks School in south-east England and working with children with PMLD is a 'passion' for her: 'My role is to give a quality of life to our youngsters that makes every minute of their waking life valuable. We have expectations of *all our children, no matter who they are*, and I mean to include children with life-limiting conditions in that. Let them be?! What right do I have to let them be? I am an educationalist – how do I know what's possible if I and others don't do everything to facilitate that? We won't know unless we make every effort to encourage our children.'

Muriel looks for the slightest sign of progress – whether a 'teeny raising of the eyebrow' or 'the facial grimace that isn't epilepsy', and above all she is looking for some sign that a child is acknowledging another human being in some way: 'If I've seen that there may be a capacity in that youngster to do a teeny bit more, however teeny, however minute – maybe just to lift a finger – then it actually moves them on. It gives them more opportunities to experience the world. We have awakened them so as to welcome them into our world. And if I can see some sign of that, some sign of acknowledgement then that gives me a sense of hope.'

Muriel's determination that any child should be welcomed into the world is inspiring, and stems from a rock-solid belief in all her children. What is the nature of this belief, more exactly?

We might believe that some child has the capability to lift her finger now; or, if not now, then in the near future; or, if not in the near future, then at some later point, given suitable therapy and encouragement. This is a belief about what someone can do or will be able to do in the future; it is a belief about a matter of fact – can she or can't she, will she or won't she? But it is also a belief that looks to what is possible in the future, and what is possible in the future will depend on how much we are encouraging and supportive of the child's development between now and then.

We might also believe that a child is precious, and certainly no less precious than anyone else because she happens to have PMLD. The subject of this belief is not only in the first instance any physical or mental attributes of the child – though these may help to explain why we believe what we do; rather, the subject of our belief is the *value* or *worth* of the child. We believe, for example, that a child has a 'value beyond price' or is 'precious beyond words', and precious beyond words irrespective, or largely independently of their mental and physical attributes.

And, finally, we can have belief *in* our children, in the sense that we trust in them, we believe that they are good or worthy of our love; that if we care for and look after them they won't let us down or abuse our trust. Children with profound disabilities are, perhaps, *especially* trustworthy – being without guile or deceit; as Rameen, mother of Usama, reminds us, 'These children are genuine; they don't hide their feelings – they're not two-faced.'

5 Finding words

Some teachers find it easy to talk about why their pupils matter so much to them. Jean Baker, who teaches at Christ Church School, finds her work so worthwhile because of how much she loves the children she is surrounded by, and for reasons that Rameen would recognise: 'I love my work. It's definitely the children. I love being around them – especially *these* children – because they completely surprise you. It's the element of *surprise* – not knowing what they can do – getting to know them – their personalities. *They all have such amazing, unique personalities.* And they are so trusting and generally happy.'

Words come easily to Beatrice Freeman, who also teaches at Christ Church. She found that working with children with PMLD put a lot else into perspective, including her time as a waitress: 'I compare my life now with my life working in a bar, serving drinks. People get stressed out about when their dinner is served. And I think, why are you getting stressed out about this? Compare this with a child having a life-threatening seizure. *A late dinner doesn't matter.*' What *does* matter are the children she now works with: 'They are precious: you don't know what's there. You never know what's coming up. If you can't express how much you care about people, you are missing out on what you are supposed to do. They give me as much as my friends. They do something new, something unexpected, something exciting.'

It is, however, not always easy to find words to explain why someone we love matters so much to us, and what it is about a loved one that makes them precious beyond price or irreplaceable. I have previously introduced George, the profoundly disabled son of Pamela, who is blind, has no language, rarely vocalises and whose only unassisted movements occur when he has one of his many seizures. Pamela reports: 'If he is in pain he will make a face, but he can't cry out, though you might get a little moaning noise. If he's soiled himself he wouldn't let you know. The way I know he's in pain or is not comfortable is not through noises but through expressions on his face.' When we talk about what's so special about George it is hard for Pamela to know what to say, as we first saw in Chapter 3: 'It's just George in himself. It's just what he gives. It's hard to put into words what he gives. He's not just a child who sits in a wheelchair – he can give so much. *It's … it's … just him … himself … what he gives … just him.'*

'Just him': what does this mean? It is sometimes said that if we are really not able to put any words to our thoughts, or to our feelings, then there is probably nothing much to say, or nothing worth saying, anyway. Gaita disagrees: there are some things about love and human preciousness that it is almost impossible to speak clearly about:

> Our sense of the preciousness of other people is connected with their power to affect us in ways we cannot fathom and in ways against which we can protect ourselves only at the cost of becoming shallow. The power of human beings to affect one another in ways beyond reason and beyond merit … is partly what yields to us that sense of human individuality which we express when we say that human beings are unique and irreplaceable. Such attachments, and the joy and the grief which they may cause, condition our sense of the preciousness of human beings. Love is the most important of them.
>
> *(2000: 26–27)*

Not many of us can put everything we care most about into words; and even if we are able to find a few words to express our feelings, the words may get nowhere near explaining what we most want to explain, which is just how precious and uniquely valuable our loved ones are. Perhaps it isn't (only) words that will get us there; but, instead, or as well, feeling, sensibility, and inarticulate awareness, along with the practical conventions and rituals we instinctually adhere to and respect, and which serve to reveal how we value and cherish those who are dear to us.

6 Concluding remarks

When Adwoa came close and looked me straight in the eye and told me, with a deep, calm pride, what an honour it was to have been the mother of Kwame, I was rooted to the spot; it was a humbling and inspiring encounter. Her voice, her testimony, as with all the voices and testimony collected here, has authority: we ought to listen, and we ought to take their words seriously. One might even think, in Adwoa's mesmeric presence, that these words tell us all we need to know. Who better to turn to than the parents and carers who have spent their lives tending to their loved ones, or the teachers whose vocation it is to work with profoundly disabled children? There is, for sure, no more valuable source of insight into the lives of people with PMLD; hence this long chapter given over to the words of those who love and know them best.

Yet if we want to think about the value and moral status not only of Kwame but also of all people with profound disabilities, and to consider these subjects from all sides, then we cannot avoid taking a step back from the testimony presented here, however powerful and compelling it is. It is necessary, also, to call upon other evidence, principles, arguments and points of view, not only or mainly for the benefit of those who already know the value of profoundly disabled people, but largely for those who have not the first idea, or who harbour doubts, or worse; and not only for our personal learning, but also to assist in the formulation of policies and laws that are better designed to respect the lives of people who have no prospect of speaking to the rest of us about who they are and why they matter. Hence the theoretical discussion to follow in the next chapter.

Points for discussion

- Do *all* people matter equally, irrespective of disability?
- How much do you get back from the children you care for? Does this depend on the presence or extent of their disabilities?
- Are some children altogether unable to reciprocate the love they receive? If so, does this affect what they are worth, to you and to other people?
- Is it possible to put into words what you feel about the value of the children or adults you look after?
- What is the role of faith and belief in your life as a carer or teacher of children with PMLD?

Notes

1 On condescension, see Cigman 2013.
2 A reference to the P scales. PI refers to the most limited set of capacities and functionings. See Chapter 2, section 4.
3 Here and elsewhere, personal correspondence.

6

VALUING PROFOUNDLY DISABLED PEOPLE

In theory

1 Introduction

Almost no one contributing to this book was in any doubt that children and adults with profound and multiple learning difficulties and disabilities are as precious as anyone else: people with PMLD are people, just like you and me; there is so much more to the value of human beings than whether we happen to be good at mathematics, communicating with others or getting around without assistance. Yet it remains a perennial question, how best to explain the value of human beings – and not only those with PMLD but all human beings – and how this is related to our moral status.

The value of a human being can be thought about from several points of view: as revealed in our personal relationships, and in our dealings with those we love and care for; as upheld in the context of morality, including the rights and duties that we think of as applying to all persons, whether or not we are personally related to them; and as asserted in the context of politics, including the rights and entitlements that attach to persons in virtue of their status as citizens and political subjects. This last is touched on elsewhere; here I discuss the value of profoundly disabled people from the moral and personal points of view (with an emphasis on the first), subjects on which those quoted in the previous chapter spoke with such eloquence.

The questions to be explored are unsettling, not only in the sense that it is difficult to know how best to answer them but also in the sense that they have been discussed in terms that readers may find objectionable. For example, some writers have compared the value of profoundly disabled human beings with the value of non-human higher primates. In order to do justice to discussions about the status of human beings, I must include some reference to these arguments. Readers who find these uncomfortable may prefer to turn away, although I encourage you not to; it is educative to confront views that are uncongenial if they force us to think further than we might otherwise about our values and why we hold them.

For his many penetrating observations, I have chosen McMahan as the chief representative of arguments that are likely to meet with disapproval, and for her personal experience and extensive philosophical writing on profound disability I have chosen Kittay as the chief representative of views that are close to those expressed by parents and carers in Chapter 5. The purpose of the chapter is to offer a brief introduction, but no more than that, to a number of arguments presented by these and other protagonists.

Moral status

There is a distinction between moral status and the value of people we may or may not care about. I may love you more than a stranger, or care for my pet dog more than a human being, but that tells us something about what I happen to value most, and that is different from the moral status that attaches to the stranger and my pet dog. We might think of moral status as a product of what we *owe* others; or that it reflects the *rights* they have which correspond to the duties *we* have. People with PMLD may be fortunate in their relations and relationships, or they may be subject to neglect and indifference. One hopes that profoundly disabled people with PMLD should not suffer from general neglect, but, if ever they do, we do not suppose that they are therefore worth less than anyone else because there is nobody else to whom they matter very much.

The moral status of a person is thought to be derived from one or more of the following: (i) the properties that are *intrinsic* to a person, such as a capacity to reason, to love someone or to respond to a piece of music; (ii) their *special relations* to others, those that go beyond the fact of belonging to the same species, and which include personal relationships and family relations; (iii) *species membership*, the fact of belonging to one and the same species – *homo sapiens*. I discuss each of these in turn.

2 Intrinsic capacities

Rationality and the will

It is a natural thought that the value of human beings resides in our defining and intrinsic characteristics. Is there some characteristic possessed by all and only human beings – something that we all have but which no other animal has? For the ancient Greeks, human beings were distinguished from other animals by their rationality. Aristotle (384–322 BC), for example, regarded human beings as essentially rational animals, and he considered reason as unique to human beings; whilst other animals are capable of sensations and appetites only human beings are capable of rational thought (Boyle forthcoming: 7). The Enlightenment philosopher Immanuel Kant (1724–1804) maintained that rational animals are the object of special moral concern.

Rational nature exists as an end in itself and all rational animals are therefore to be accorded respect (2012: 40–41). This leaves it open as to whether all human beings are rational animals, and whether any animals besides human beings have a rational nature. When we turn to contemporary philosophers, Dennett is one of many for whom rationality is a distinguishing characteristic of persons: all persons are self-conscious rational beings, capable of verbal communication, acting with intentions, and of reciprocating attitudes and behaviour shown by others (1978: 267–285).

Not everyone agrees that it is rationality, as such, that represents the defining feature of a person. For Frankfurt the concept of a person is related not only to rationality but also to the will. He distinguishes between first- and second-order desires:

> Besides wanting and choosing and being moved to do this or that, men may also want to have (or not to have) certain desires and motives. They are capable of wanting to be different, in their preferences and purposes, from what they are. Many animals appear to have the capacity for what I shall call 'first-order desires' or 'desires of the-first order,' which are simply desires to do or not to do one thing or another. No animal other than man, however, appears to have the capacity for reflective self-evaluation that is manifested in the formation of second-order desires.
>
> *(1971: 7)*

Suppose someone both wants to smoke a cigarette and wants not to smoke – he knows that smoking is bad for his health. What he most wants is that his desire not to smoke should prove stronger than his desire to smoke – his will is that he should choose not to smoke, even though he wants to. If, in the end, he lights his cigarette, he acts in conformity with his first-order desire; if he resists this temptation, and does what he wants to want, he acts in conformity with his will, and it is a choice of this second kind that Frankfurt regards as a defining characteristic of persons (ibid.: 10).

Where does this leave profoundly disabled people? Many will comfortably display the rationality and reflective evaluation described here, but not all will: the ability to decide on the basis of reasons, or critically to evaluate one's own desires, requires extensive cognitive functioning, and some people with PMLD will offer only very limited evidence of this, if that. At the same time, rationality and action in conformity with the will are not all-or-nothing capacities, and it would be a mistake to think that they are somehow 'static' among people with PMLD. Carlson emphasises the importance of potential:

> Given the historical legacy of static characterizations of mental retardation, as well as the complexities of diagnosis, definition and treatment surrounding intellectual disabilities, the issues of potential may be even *more* complicated than in the case of a normal infant. Moreover, there is ample evidence to suggest that even the most profoundly intellectually disabled individual can experience some forms of development.
>
> *(2010: 141)*

The testimony presented in Chapter 5, and throughout this book, lends substantial support to Carlson's last statement. Even so, should we elect to prize rationality and the rational will above all other human characteristics – as the distinguishing characteristics of human beings and a primary source of human value – then, however much we allow for potential, some profoundly disabled people are likely not to be accorded the same status and worth as most other people. Nor will they be alone in this, since the cognitive powers of many older people decline to the point that they would also struggle to meet any 'rationality' test.

Love and affection

Perhaps what is most valuable about human beings is not rationality but just what featured most vividly in the previous chapter: the capacity to love and to be loved, and to bring joy or a smile into people's lives. This is Kittay's view, expressed here in a passage about her profoundly disabled daughter:

> She has no measurable IQ ... Most capacities she will not develop at all. Is she then a 'vegetable'? The term is ludicrous when applied to Sesha because there is nothing vegetative about her. She is fully a human, not a vegetable. Given the scope and breadth of human possibilities and capacities, she occupies a limited spectrum, but she inhabits it fully because she has the most important faculty of all. The capacities for love and for happiness. These allow those of us who care for her, who love her, who have been entrusted with her well-being to form deep and abiding attachments to her. Sesha's coin and currency is love. That is what she wishes to receive and that is what she reciprocates in spades.
>
> *(1999: 151–152)*

This seems to move in a direction that is congenial for people with PMLD. A person with no measurable IQ may yet be unusually sensitive, joyous and caring, and, thereby, make an inestimable contribution to the lives of other people. Of course, this will not be true of every profoundly disabled person; Sam and Nadifa, discussed previously, often give no evidence, or almost no evidence, that any response of theirs is a response to human care and affection. But there is a more significant problem; for if, nevertheless, we maintain that the capacity for love and care is a significant source of moral status, we then run into the question of what we should say about some non-human animals. There are humans who love their pets and other animals more than they do any other humans; and some pets – for example, the two dogs adopted by Pitcher and his partner – may reciprocate:

> They showed this constantly, in countless ways. ... We loved them with all our hearts ... and they loved us, too, completely, no holds barred ... They were our surrogate children. ... Naturally the love of one's dog cannot be as deep and rich as the love of one's child, but it can be in some ways just as

intense. For example, our concern for the welfare of Lupa and Remus was, I believe, as strong as a devoted father's for his child's.

(Quoted in McMahan 2005: 364)

Kittay rejects any suggestion that in speaking about the love of humans and the love of dogs we are talking about the same thing:

> I am no stranger to a beloved animal. I have had dogs I have loved, dogs I have mourned for. But as dog lovers who become parents can tell you, much as we adore our hounds, there is no comparison between the feelings for a beloved child of normal capacities and those for a beloved canine. And I can tell you that there is also no comparison when that child has intellectual disabilities.
>
> *(2010: 397)*

Kittay's testimony to her love for her daughter is arresting and authoritative, as is similar testimony presented elsewhere in this book; but then so too is Pitcher's account of his relationship with his dogs. Nor can we assume that our psychological reactions to others should determine what our reactions ought to be. The fact that a relation with someone may elicit either love and affection or indifference and unconcern does not show that the presence of the relation *justifies* any of these responses. If it did we would be forced to conclude that the feelings and claims of neglectful, cruel or indifferent parents were also justified, and that would amount to an endorsement of neglect, cruelty and indifference. The fact that one person has feelings of one kind towards another cannot, either by itself or as emerging from a special relationship, justify either those feelings or a claim about the moral status of the person they are directed towards (McMahan 2002: 220).

Perhaps love and other forms of cherishing are to be regarded not only as 'feelings' or other psychological states, but also as containing properties that reveal something of what is valuable about us; perhaps they even represent a *source* of value. Suggestions of this kind are pursued elsewhere, but if they are to prove credible, it will be necessary to explain why love has the property of revealing value in human beings, whilst hatred or indifference, for example, do not; and we will also need to explain *how* it is that love, as such, can serve as a source of value, let alone moral status, and where that leaves people who are unloved and forgotten about.

Not only intrinsic capacities

Kittay does not believe that our moral responsibilities should be determined by details of our intrinsic human capacities:

> Every parent needs schools and other institutions to ensure that her child can develop her capacities, *whatever those capacities may be* ... If [any philosophers] claim to honor my relationship to my child and to grant its moral significance, then they cannot with any consistency grant the means to fulfil parental

obligations to one parent and deny them to another parent based on some set of features of the child, for these are what all parents need to fulfil their ethical responsibilities to their children *regardless* of their capacities and needs.

(2010: 410; italics added)

'Regardless' can be read as 'irrespective of', which implies that we can give an account of our responsibilities which is in no way related to the capacity and needs of the child. That is too strong. The responsibility of parents towards an anencephalic infant with no prospect of gaining consciousness is not the same as the responsibility they have towards a healthy child. Kittay would not want to claim that there is an obligation on anyone, including parents, to ensure that the anencephalic child has access to a school. Hence, not *all* parental responsibilities towards their children can be determined without *any* reference to intrinsic properties.

'Regardless' might be interpreted more liberally to imply, not that we need make no reference to intrinsic capacities, but that these capacities do not by themselves determine what our moral responsibilities are. The capacities of a lissencephalic child are greatly less than those of a child without disabilities but it does not follow that the obligation to provide adequate healthcare for the first child is any less urgent than it is for the second. We may have an obligation to provide healthcare so long as it is established that the child has *some* health-related needs, provided only that these meet a threshold which marks a capacity to respond and benefit. If this is right, then our moral responsibilities – at least in this case – are sensitive to some details of our intrinsic properties, but certainly not to all.

What else besides or in addition to our intrinsic properties could help explain our value and moral status? For many writers it is important that we belong to a human community, and that we are bound up in a network of relations and relationships.

3 Relations and relationships

People with profound disabilities are *related* to other people, including members of their family, and they have *relationships* with others, such as their carers and teachers. Some of our relations are morally significant: a mother has reasons to treat her child differently from other children just because this child is hers. These reasons are 'agent-relative' – they apply to her, as the mother of her child, and not to people generally – whilst reasons that apply to people generally, and not only to those involved in special relations, are 'agent-neutral'. The family represents an example of social relations which are a source of special reasons for the care and protection owed to relatives; and since we are all some mother's child (Kittay 2010: 412), we are all related to at least one other person who has a special reason for taking care of us.

McMahan acknowledges that we have agent-relative moral reasons for how we treat members of our family, including family members with profound disabilities:

The people who are closely related to severely retarded human beings have special reasons to protect and care for them and are typically strongly and appropriately motivated by love and compassion to do so. And the rest of us are morally bound to respect these people's feelings and commitments.

(2002: 232)

We should respect the commitments of parents because of *their* special relations with profoundly disabled children, an obligation which does not depend on *our* having special relations with those carers (ibid.). Kittay has an objection to this argument, which comes down to the claim that 'no child is simply the parent's own private matter':

> Foremost is the need that the wider society recognise the worth and worthiness of the child. It is incoherent to grant the special relationship I have with my daughter and then to turn around and say, 'But that daughter has no moral hold on anyone but her parent.' Her parent cannot fulfil her role as parent, unless others also have an acknowledged moral responsibility to the child – a moral responsibility on a par with the one it has to anyone's child.

(2010: 410)

Kittay asks that recognition of a child's worth should extend beyond her parents, but this cannot be established on the basis of a special relationship alone. Why should anyone else acknowledge your worth as a child, simply because you are the apple of your mother's eye? This relationship may be a matter of indifference to anyone other than you and your mother. In any case, if the source of moral value derived from our relationships, it would follow that unloved orphans and people without any relationships to speak of would have lesser moral status, as compared to family members and those in healthy relationships. It would be perverse to compound the predicament of isolated people by suggesting that they are worth less just because they have no remaining family members and there is no one else who cares for them.

Kittay suggests that it is *incoherent* to grant that she has a special relationship with her daughter whilst denying that her daughter has a moral hold on anyone else. But we are not compelled to grant that you have a moral hold on anyone other than your mother even if we allow that you have a moral hold on her. The apple of one mother's eye was once Adolf Hitler. In this case we might have acknowledged the relationship, but not – at any rate, towards the end of his life – that this should have imposed anything more than minimal obligations on the rest of us. Any duties owed to the adult Hitler who had committed crimes against humanity were owed in virtue of his status as a human being; we owed him, perhaps, some minimal level of respect (we shouldn't torture him), but we owed him nothing further simply because his mother doted on him.

Kittay's principal complaint is against any suggestion that concern for her daughter arises out of concern for her as the mother:

> [I]t is not for *my* sake that I want my child recognised. It is for *her* sake. That is the nature of the parental relationship. It's not that I want people to care about Sesha because I care about her. It's that I cannot give her the care it is

> my duty to provide if others do not respect her as a being worthy of the same
> care as is due to any child.
>
> *(2010: 410)*

If recognition is owed for Sesha's sake, and not her mother's, recognition is owed in virtue of properties that are intrinsic to Sesha; if, however, recognition is owed to Sesha as a condition of her mother caring for her, then recognition is owed not only in virtue of Sesha's worth but also in virtue of her mother's duty of care. The former option makes no appeal to special relations (as between mother and daughter), whilst the latter singles out any relations implicit in a duty of care. Although there is truth in the claim that any recognition is for *Sesha*'s sake, it may turn out that, in order to understand this, we must appeal both to her intrinsic properties and to facts about how she is related to others.

In keeping with this last suggestion, I will consider whether the value we attribute to human beings is in any way a reflection of how and whether we choose to accept them into our community. Boddington and Podpadec discuss a case where the appearance of a child, Betsy, had an impact on her treatment, for her facial features were in some people's eyes unattractive and this counted against her receiving care (1991: 184).[1] Her parents did not think that they could look after her, and Betsy faced a bleak and institutionalised future. Moreover, the fact that 'Betsy [was perceived to have had] rather peculiarly repulsive features led the parents to fear that she would receive particularly poor care.' Betsy's condition subsequently deteriorated, her parents decided against surgery, and she died (Beauchamp and Childress 1983 quoted in Boddington and Podpadec 1991: 184).

For Boddington and Podpadec the fate of Betsy illustrates the fact that how we value and treat someone reflects not only their intrinsic qualities, but also our reactions to those qualities, including whether we are disposed to welcome or ostracise the person whose qualities they are. A person may be rejected from her community, or deemed less valuable than someone else, not simply because she has some unusual facial features, but also because a negative reaction to her appearance has an influence on her status and perceived worth. Betsy's status reflects a judgement that she is somehow worth less than others, in part because she is seen as unattractive or repulsive, and this judgement has a bearing on the decision whether to withhold life-saving medical treatment.

Our conception of others as persons may therefore incorporate judgements about what we prize and esteem, dislike and reject. And such value judgements as these have a relational aspect; they tend to express or presuppose views on whether someone is to be regarded as belonging to our community, or as having the status of a fully equal member of our society (Boddington and Podpadec 1991:187).

4 Species membership

In testimony presented elsewhere, particularly about children whose disabilities are especially profound, carers talk not only about the distinctive characteristics of one child or another, but also about the basic fact that, whatever else we may say, he or she is *a human being*, is *one of us*, is *our fellow creature*. These thoughts have been discussed by philosophers.

Kittay (2009) writes that species membership is important to human beings because we all share common interests, hopes and fears, and also sensual and emotional experiences, and ways of knowing the world and each other. Stephen Mulhall takes a similar view:

> To see another as a human being is to see her as a fellow-creature. … We do not strive (when we do strive) to treat human infants and children, the senile and the severely disabled as fully human because we mistakenly attribute capacities to them that they lack, or because we are blind to the merely biological significance of a species boundary. We do it (when we do) because they are fellow human beings, embodied creatures who will come to share, or have already shared, in our common life, or whose inability to do so is a result of the shocks and ills to which all human flesh and blood is heir – because there but for the grace of God go I.
>
> *(2002: 18)*

These thoughts express what many carers think about people with profound learning difficulties. But not everyone is persuaded. McMahan, for example, is not. He suggests that the forms of common life described here do not include people with radical cognitive impairments; they 'do not, and cannot, share our language, culture, ways of knowing, and so on' (2005: 363). There are, of course, examples of 'participation' in a common human life that allow for the inclusion of profoundly disabled people, as in the contexts of the families and schools described throughout this book. And Tim Webb, Director of Oily Cart, makes a similar point (in Chapter 2) when he asserts that the children he works with themselves participate in his theatre – they are part of the spectacle and the performance, even whilst having only the most limited awareness of this. McMahan might acknowledge that 'participation' can apply to many types of activity but he would go on to say that, if we allow for a generous reading of 'participation', including cases in which the cognitive demands on human beings are minimal, then exactly the same kind of participation might extend to cognitively advanced non-human animals. McMahan points out that Pitcher's dogs entered deeply into their keepers' lives and that this is an example of participation more extensive than some human beings are capable of, and not only some profoundly disabled human beings but also persons who exhibit the severest forms of psychopathy or who are in the last stages of dementia (2005: 364–365).

Mulhall refers to 'severely disabled' people as our fellow embodied human beings and one aspect of embodiment is the human face. The face is often thought of as providing a window into the soul; or perhaps Wittgenstein's inverted formula is more accurate, that 'the face is the soul of the body' (1998: 23). Either way, in her account of intellectual disability Carlson denies that it is in any way arbitrary to insist on the importance of an appeal to the human face as part of our humanity, and as revealing something of what distinguishes the claims of human beings from other animals (2010: 154). McMahan, however, remains unimpressed by any idea that 'all human beings, including the radically cognitively impaired, are our fellow creatures, and thus make a claim on us, simply because they *look like us*, (2005: 363).

The idea of a fellow creature is discussed in the work of Diamond, who emphasises the role of imagination in thinking about the distinctive value of human life (1991: 35–62). She writes of 'our imaginative sense of what it is to be human,' and our 'imaginative sense of human life' (ibid.: 43, 56, 58); our imagination shows up the 'otherness' of animal life, and this contrasts with 'human boundness, (ibid.: 41, 55):

> The sense of mystery surrounding our lives, the feeling of solidarity in mysterious origin and uncertain fate: this binds us to each other ... there is the possibility of deep moral concern for retarded people, in which they are seen as having, however incomprehensible we may find it, a human fate, as much as anyone else's. They are seen as with us in being human, where that is understood not in a biological sense, but imaginatively. Someone may be very touched by the response of a severely retarded person to music; and there may be in that being touched an imaginative sense of shared humanity.
>
> *(Ibid.: 55)*

The appeal to the imagination is frequently made in these pages: we should always try to imagine what children with PMLD are capable of, and assume that they 'can' rather than that they 'cannot'; we can never be absolutely certain what someone might be able to do, or think, or understand, and we should therefore constantly exercise an 'imaginative charity' towards others. But there are sceptics for whom thoughts of this kind are quite obscure. Whilst Diamond writes of how imagination can reveal the importance of having a human life to lead, McMahan is moved to comment that 'I am not the only one whose imagination does not seem to be up to the task of apprehending the significance of having a human life to lead' (2005: 371). What, he asks, does it mean to speak of 'having a human life to lead'? Diamond would insist that, whilst someone may be deprived of many distinctively human capacities, a human life without these capacities is, nevertheless, a human life – 'it just *is* what his having a human life to lead has been' (1991: 59). McMahan would not be convinced, but Diamond's thoughts are shared by many people we hear from throughout this book.

Diamond (1991) offers one example of what may be involved in our 'sense of shared humanity' – namely, our being moved by how someone who is profoundly disabled responds to music. In Chapter 2 we looked not only at how music is listened to but also at how it is played by people with profound disabilities. Music reveals ability and potential that might not be thought possible if we looked only at someone's capacity for verbal communication and problem solving. It also allows for communion between listeners, and between players and listeners. A favoured melody, rhythm or sound world is food for the soul, and allows one person to reach out to or connect with another. This is why music can remind us of someone's humanity and contribute to a sense of human fellowship – two themes repeatedly discussed by those who write about profound disability and those who live with it (Ockleford 2008; Ansdell 2014).

However, it would be dogmatic to assert that no animals besides human beings are capable of an aesthetic response to music; and, if there are any such animals, we are left with the question what an aesthetic capacity implies for *their* moral status, and why that is different – if it is different – from the status of human beings, whether profoundly disabled or otherwise (McMahan 2005: 372).

5 Concluding remarks

The questions discussed in this chapter are difficult. This is not because, or solely because, we are thinking about people with profound disabilities; they are difficult because it is not easy to give a good explanation of *anyone's* value and moral status, whoever they may be. And now we know so much more about the capacities of other animals, it is becoming harder to say why the value of all human beings is something over and above the value of all animals that are not human.

I have looked at how we might want to account for the moral status of profoundly disabled people, including an appeal to intrinsic qualities, relations and relationships and the fact that someone is a fellow member of the human species. Perhaps we should say something about all three of these considerations, but not everything we might want to say about someone's intrinsic qualities is compatible with what we might want to say about their relationships, or their belonging to the human species. If, for example, what ultimately matters from a moral point of view is that someone should have the *capacity* for love and for being loved, then their status should be unaffected by whether they are blessed with many or few relations and relationships. If, however, what ultimately matters is simply that we are all 'our fellow creatures', in virtue of belonging to the same species, then it should make no difference whether our capacities are either extensive or so limited that we cannot meet even our most basic needs.

I have included some uncomfortable thoughts in this chapter, about the basis on which we value the lives of human beings and other animals, and these merit respectful attention, to say the least. At the same time we have been invited to consider that at least some part of what matters most about human beings is determined not by many of the details of their capabilities, or by the extent of family relations and the number of their relationships; rather, that it lies in the fact that human beings are a source and object of love, or that they are *capable* of love, or even that we can *imagine* that they are capable of love; and in the fact that each person – and each person with profound disabilities – has qualities and a personality that are uniquely theirs, and who by their smiles and good nature offer as much to those who care for them as anyone else – and sometimes more. These, at any rate, are possibilities that emerge from some of the reflections offered in this chapter, and practically all of the testimony presented in the last. These too deserve serious consideration, albeit under the gaze of critics who need persuading that this is not merely an exercise in wishful and confused thinking.

Points for discussion

* To what extent is someone's moral status dependent on either their relations and relationships or the fact of belonging to the human species?
* How is a person's moral status related to their intrinsic properties (if at all)?
* Do all human beings have either a special value or moral status, over and above those of other animals, irrespective of how their capacities compare?
* In what sense, if any, does the value of a person lie in 'the eye of the beholder'?

Note

1   The case is discussed in Beauchamp and Childress 1983: 309–310.

7

RESPECT AND HUMAN DIGNITY

1 Introduction

Most of us believe that all human beings have dignity – human dignity – and that each of us should be treated with a basic respect. Treatment that violates human dignity or is incompatible with a basic respect for human beings is thought of as degrading or inhuman, and is absolutely prohibited in many of the world's jurisdictions. But what exactly is 'human dignity' and what do we mean when we say that everyone ought to be treated with respect?

Once we raise these questions others swiftly follow: is human dignity *intrinsic* to human beings, a property that we have in the same way that we are of a certain height and weight? Or is dignity something we *accord* to a person in virtue of how we behave towards them, as when we treat someone with dignity? To what extent are our ideas of dignity and respect imbued with *cultural norms*, which help to determine whether practices previously deemed compatible with human dignity remain so today?

Each question raises difficult issues, and these are compounded if the human beings whose dignity is in question are not able to think or talk about these subjects for themselves. This applies to many people with profound learning difficulties, who, as recipients of treatment or participants in practices that we would deem consonant with or inimical to human dignity, may not experience the treatment or practices under that description, or anything like it.

Whilst there is general agreement that respecting others, and respect for their human dignity in particular, are precepts that should guide our behaviour at all times, it is not always clear what the practical and theoretical implications of these precepts are. A practical example: is it inimical to the dignity of a pupil if a teacher talks over her head, if the pupil is not herself aware of anything being done to her that she minds about? A theoretical example: does respect for a person imply that we should always seek to promote her independence, if the person has a life-limiting condition, is in a lot of pain, and finds most pleasure from routines she knows well and is comfortable with?

Section 2 includes examples of how teachers and carers talk about treating someone with respect; in section 3 I look at what the basis of dignity and respect might be; in section 4 I explore the idea that respect for a person essentially involves making an effort to see the world from their point of view; and in section 5 I look at various ways in which we can look at someone, either as a person, or as someone less than a person. Finally, in section 6, I explore why it matters that someone with PMLD should be seen as a person, including the importance of their being acknowledged by and connected to other people.

2 Treating people with respect

For some people it goes without saying that the children they live and work with are owed the same respect as anyone else. Here are some introductory examples about people with profound disabilities, and also about just one of the many areas – toileting – in which it is easy for dignity to become compromised.

'They're still human beings, they're still children'

Leonda Ratcliffe is a 54-year-old Jamaican mother of two children, and a support assistant at St Peter's School. It is especially important to Leonda that the children with PMLD she works with are human beings, however much they may differ in their capabilities from other people: 'They can't help the way they are, but still, they're the same as anyone else. You mustn't treat them any differently from anyone else – they're still human beings, they're still children. If it was me, I'd want to be treated like I treat them. I'd want the same respect as I give to others. And it doesn't cost anything to be nice to people.'

One way of failing to respect people is to patronise them, something that Leonda seeks to avoid: 'I just talk to the children with PMLD the same as I talk to you. I don't see why I should talk to them any differently. Some people "baby them" too much. You don't need to do that.'

In the same vein Leonda teaches her own children that children with PMLD are children too: 'I teach my children: "Children with PMLD are the same as you. They didn't ask to be born with disabilities. You should treat them the same." My children have learned to respect special needs children as much as anyone else.'

Sian Peterson is a senior support assistant at Alfred Marks School. For Sian, as with Leonda, showing respect for children with PMLD is to see them, fundamentally, as just like any other children: 'My friend saw how I interact with her son. I didn't treat her disabled son any differently to her other children – I saw her son as 'him', and 'it' – the disability – didn't make any difference. Here, at Alfred Marks, you don't treat the children any differently. Obviously they have complex needs. But I look at them as children as I do my other children – but obviously needing a lot more care and time.'

And as she looks at the children in her school just as she might look at any other children so Sian talks to them in the same way too, including those who are very sick: 'I believe that you show a child with PMLD the same dignity and respect as you would any other child. If a child is very weak, someone might say, "Oh God, they've been sick again!", rather than saying something more kindly, more understanding. One child I had been working with – aged 3 – was sick almost every day. But that didn't matter to me; that was the way he was. I'm very accepting. I take someone as they are.'

Toileting

One domain in which dignity may be variously lost, compromised or violated is that of basic human functioning – eating and drinking, sexual behaviour, defecation and so on. These human activities are the subject of cultural norms that vary markedly from one society to another, and we cannot, therefore, talk about what dignity and respect involves without talking about the cultures and places that people inhabit and live in. Yet in one case, catering to the basic needs of children with PMLD living in England in the twenty-first century, the thoughts and beliefs of carers and teachers are remarkably consistent. Toileting is just one example of many that might have been included here, but the remarks below serve to bring out details in behaviour and attitudes which illustrate a fundamental respect for people whose dignity might otherwise be lost sight of.

Judith Appleby, a teacher at the Litster School, describes how she talks with and behaves towards a child who has soiled himself. She treats him as she might treat anyone else; she doesn't talk over his head or treat him as someone who doesn't understand anything she is saying: 'I might say to a child, "Oh my God – you've done a really smelly poo!" I'd say this because we deal with this all the time. But I *wouldn't* go over someone's head and say, "Oh my God *he's* done a really smell poo!" In the first case I am discussing this with the child – I'm not patronising him. In the second case you are going over his head. You don't have to treat children like little feathers. You can still just chat to them even if they don't understand your language. But I'm talking to them, making them feel like we're in this together rather than my just pushing people around. I don't treat the children as if they are babies. In that case you *could* say to another adult, "He's done a really smelly poo." But I wouldn't say this about the children here in this school. You treat the poo as something you are going to deal with together. And you treat this as if it isn't a chore. I do it for them so that they are not left sitting in it. And it's something I *can* do and they *can't* – it's not like I am doing them a favour. I don't want them to think that I think: "Oh my God you have done this horrible thing." Of course we both prefer that they could do it for themselves. But if we do it together it's not like I'm resenting the fact that they're doing something that they can't help and which, anyway, everyone does.'

Besides not patronising someone – treating him like a 'little feather' – respect may take the form of refusing to be taken up with the animalistic and off-putting aspect of human functioning, and attuning oneself to the person that the human animal also is. In her published work Corbett describes how one of her students, John, a 16 year old with Down's syndrome and no speech, returned from a coach trip covered in his own excrement:

> It seemed to me that it should be someone he both knew and trusted who should clean him up. So I took him to the bathroom area and I think we actually ended up in the shower together, making the whole cleaning up process a bit of a laugh ... I tried to concentrate upon the person I liked and not the unpleasant nature of the task ... For me, in this context, there was no division between sitting at tables in the classroom using a variety of teaching aids and taking the student to the toilet and helping them at mealtimes. If our purpose was to teach them that they are valued people, then every aspect of our daily interaction was part of that teaching.
>
> *(1992: 237–238)*

When toileting a child, Sian Peterson at Alfred Marks takes care to communicate using body signs, so that there are no surprises – the child knows what is about to happen and is not simply 'thrust into a toilet': 'You have to treat them with the dignity and respect you would show to any child, no matter if they are disabled or able bodied. Say if I'm taking a child to the toilet I'll do body signs on them. As you speak, "Are you ready to go to the toilet?" you have a different touch for every word – like the Makaton signing but this is on the body. So I take them into the bathroom and make sure that the door is closed and then hoist them on to the toilet, using a touch cue. Then you toilet the child, put them back in the hoist, using the touch cue. And with an able-bodied child you wouldn't just thrust them into the toilet without telling them what you are doing. And you wouldn't leave the bathroom door wide open.'

Toileting is just one of countless examples in which dignity may be retained or lost depending on how a person is treated, handled, looked at, spoken to or otherwise communicated with. I will explore the practices and perceptions of carers throughout this chapter, but at this point it is worth pausing to look at the *reasons* for treating people with dignity and respect.

3 Justifying respect

Why should we treat a human being with respect? Why suppose that human beings have what we call 'human dignity'? Numerous answers are offered in response to these questions. I will mention three and concentrate on just one, the importance of the human point of view.

Human reason

Many philosophers find the basis for our human dignity as lying in our capacity for rationality. According to a tradition going back to the Stoics, every human being has dignity just in virtue of having rational capacities, and the dignity of reason is worthy of respect wherever it is found. As we saw in Chapter 6, Kant held that *all* rational animals should be respected, and he expressed this requirement in his famous 'Formula of Humanity':

> So act that you use humanity, whether in your own person or in the person of any other, always at the same time as an end, never merely as a means.
>
> *(2012: 41)*

We should always treat a person as an end in herself, never merely as a means to our own ends. Why? Kant writes that 'the ground of this principle is: *rational nature exists as an end it itself*' (2012: 41). Most people have a rational will; that is, an ability to reflect on and moderate their appetites and impulses by means of rational deliberation and autonomous choice.

Kant says that we should respect all creatures that have a rational nature. But some people with PMLD have only the most limited capacity for rational and autonomous behaviour, and for some people, and by no means only those with PMLD, this capacity has become vanishingly small. Not everyone, perhaps, possesses a rational nature, and certainly not to the same extent. These people are vulnerable to the view that they might somehow not merit the respect owed to those possessing 'the dignity of reason'.

Love and affection

Just as in the discussion about human worth, we might ask at this point: why assume that rationality is the only capacity that can account for human dignity? What about the capacity for fellowship between human beings? When Midgley writes that 'what makes creatures our fellow beings, entitled to basic consideration, is surely not intellectual capacity but emotional fellowship' (1985: 60), she is expressing a view frequently voiced by writers and practitioners. Kittay invites us to consider a person whose rational capacities are difficult to determine owing to an inability to communicate and related cognitive impairments, yet who has the capacity 'to enjoy life, to share her joy through her smiles and laughter, to embrace those who show her love, and to bring joy to all whose lives she touches' (2005: 123). Besides exaggerating the relationship between dignity and rationality, Kittay alleges that philosophers tend to understate the role of other capacities in our moral life:

> capacities that we would want to encourage in the members of a moral community, such as giving care and responding appropriately to care, empathy, and fellow feeling; a sense of what is harmonious and loving; and a capacity for kindness and appreciation of those who are kind.
>
> *(Ibid.)*

In a similar vein Martha Nussbaum argues for an approach to understanding human dignity that takes in much more than the capacity to reason:

> [F]ull and equal human dignity is possessed by any child of human parents who has any of an open-ended disjunction of basic capabilities for major human life-activities … we would include a range of children and adults with severe mental difficulties, some of whom are capable of love and care but not of reading and writing, some of whom are capable of reading and writing but severely challenged in the area of social interaction.
>
> *(2008: 363)*

Although some profoundly disabled people have only limited rationality, they may have a boundless capacity for activities which are quintessentially human. Time and again parents and teachers talk about the joy and love they find in the children they look after, which is no less and often a good deal more than they find in people whose cognitive powers are more extensive. The joy and love offered by one child often inspires the same in others, and can teach us something about the importance of what we care about – including the value of human beings and their relationships. These are reasons for respecting someone, and suggest, perhaps, a basis for human dignity as lying in our capacity to love and develop relationships with other human beings.

The human point of view

In his discussion of respect, Williams notes that an effort is required to look at the world from the 'human point of view': this invites us to make a distinction between, on the one hand, a group of persons with profound learning difficulties, and, on the other, each of its members who as individuals have their own experience of disability. What is involved might be explained by saying that:

> [e]ach man is owed an effort at identification: that he should not be regarded as the surface to which a certain label can be applied, but one should try to see the world (including the label) from his point of view.
>
> *(Williams 1973: 236)*

Respect requires that we do more than simply categorise people as profoundly disabled, and that we refrain from writing people off as imbeciles or even just as 'profoundly disabled'. Rather, we are to make an effort to look at the world from their point of view; to enquire into what it is like for someone to live their life, to succeed in taking three assisted steps rather than yesterday's two, to struggle with the constraints that prevent or jeopardise communication. Pedagogy for children with severe and profound learning difficulties is of a piece with this requirement, as being both child-centred and seeking to connect with the interests and understanding of each learner (Corbett and Norwich 1999: 125). Corbett observes that many teachers working in the special school sector develop a caring pedagogy resting on 'insight into the nuances of each individual child's behaviour patterns and means of communicating' (ibid.: 132).

The suggestion is that respect for profoundly disabled people requires that we make an effort to see the world from their point of view. But why is anyone owed an effort at identification? Williams argues that the injunction is '[b]ased on, though not of course fully explained by, the notion that men are conscious beings who necessarily have intentions and purposes and see what they are doing in a certain light' (1973: 236–237). Profoundly disabled people may be unable to speak or contribute to a process of rational argument, but even when these capacities are absent, they remain conscious agents, whose acts reveal human intentions and purposes, and they are, or, very often they are, aware of those acts under some description. If Williams provides a basis for respecting people, then it is a basis for respecting profoundly disabled people. The remainder of this chapter is taken up with an exploration of what it means to identify with another person and to see the world from their point of view, and why any of this matters.

4 Seeing humans

Johnny

What is involved in recognising someone as a person? In their discussion of personhood, Boddington and Podpadec quote powerful testimony from David Goode, a young American researcher taken on a tour of a hospital for people with learning difficulties:

> I walked toward the bed and peeked over the edge and was as intensely horrified as I have ever been in my life at what I saw. A huge head, later I was told over 40 pounds, attached to this stunted body. Horrible bedsores covered what appeared for a moment as an almost unreal monstrosity – like a Hollywood inspired nightmare … I immediately became nauseous and broke out in a cold sweat and light headedness … A nurse must have seen me. She miraculously appeared, grabbed my arm and talked in a calm and reassuring manner … A few moments after this incident a young physician on the ward told me this man was 'hydrocephalic' and had been born before the invention of the shunt operation which prevents the accumulation of cerebral-spinal fluid and enlargement of the skull. In this case the head had grown so large that inter-cranial pressure rendered the person deaf, blind, completely paralysed and without a behavioural repertoire of measurable (or otherwise) signs of intelligence … The clinical profile was hopeless – no possibility existed for remediation … the person as low functioning as one could find. It was not till I got back … and listened to the audio tape of my ward tour that I was able to hear what the nurse had been saying to me. It went like this: 'Oh, I see you've found Johnny, my favourite. He's been here three and a half years and he's my special favourite. He's eighteen and I'm his mommy during the day. I wake him when I come on shift, wash him and dress him. We have our routines … He loves rock and roll, I usually open the window up so it's bright and put the music on loud. He loves when I take his hands and clap them to the beat. He

has his likes and dislikes you know ...' As I listened I could only ask myself, what happened to the person I had seen? This description did not 'jive' ... a deafblind, completely paralysed, grotesquely hydrocephalic person with 'likes and dislikes', his own routines and who someone calls her 'favourite'?

(Boddington and Podpadec 1991: 185–186, quoting Goode 1984: 229–230)

Three kinds of social relationships are in evidence here: a stranger looks on Johnny as a 'monster or object of disgust', whilst the doctor sees him in negative diagnostic terms, as 'essentially and irremediably flawed' and 'without positive prognoses'. Neither Goode nor the doctor see Johnny as the nurse sees Johnny: having come to know him over several years, she was able to relate to him as a person, and as someone capable of human interaction (Boddington and Podpadec 1991: 186).

There are great differences between some ways of looking at people and others; I will explore ways of seeing and regarding people and how this is related to respect and human dignity.

Attending to a person

It is helpful to begin by considering what can happen if we fail to respect someone. Lack of respect is elucidated by Frankfurt as consisting in:

the circumstance that some important fact about the person is not properly attended to or is not taken appropriately into account. In other words, the person is dealt with as though he is not what he actually is. The implications of significant features of his life are overlooked or denied. Pertinent aspects of how things are with him are treated as though they had no reality. It is as though, because he is denied suitable respect, his very existence is reduced.

(1999: 152–153)

There is no more common charge levelled against able-bodied people than that their conception of disability tends to exaggeration, so that the impairment is taken to be more disabling than the facts of disability themselves warrant. Or the mistake is one of indiscrimination in perception, taking one form of disability to be much like another. Silvers writes that, 'our aversion to the very idea of being disabled forestalls our understanding the disabled from their perspective' (1995: 37) a remark elaborated upon by Tetzchner and Jensen:

many professionals' perception of people with disability seems to be based on the fear they experience when they think of how it would be like to be in a similar situation. This may create a false belief of empathy and of being able to evaluate what a good life is for that other person. This false belief increases the probability that the professional's own view will be attributed to people with a disability as if they did not have their own life.

(1999: 456–457)

There are several ways in which 'some important fact about the person is not properly attended to'. Of course, profoundly disabled people face the prospect of simply being *overlooked*, and in this case we do not see them at all – either their person or their disability. Whilst this is a common fate, I am interested here in cases in which people *are* seen by others, but in ways that are in one way or another incompatible with what respect requires.

When we see profoundly disabled people as *sub-human* we see them as stigmatised; that is, as Margalit puts it, we see a physical 'anomaly' as a sign of a defect in their humanity:

> stigmata serve as marks of Cain upon people's very humanity. Bearers of a stigma appear to their surroundings as bearers of a label that makes them seem less human.
>
> *(1996: 103–104)*

A profoundly disabled person may be seen as a human being, but as a stigmatised and flawed human being. She is seen thus when all or most attention is on the disability, none or little on the person who is disabled.

I introduced Rameen Gurmani and Usama, her profoundly disabled 6-year-old son in Chapter 5. Not everyone in the family was able to accept that Usama had learning difficulties. Rameen reports that: 'They just found it difficult to accept, though I think they knew in their hearts. Perhaps they were ashamed. They couldn't get used to Usama being different. My mother in law was always looking for a reason why Usama might stay at home rather than join us all at a family gathering.'

Usama is 'different' – 'flawed' – and is neither recognised nor accepted as 'one of us'. She is stigmatised and rejected.

One manifestation of looking on someone as different and worth less is to (feel free to) stare at him. Since staring at someone is generally felt to be intrusive and insulting, those who stare suggest by their behaviour that they do not regard the person as deserving of respectful attention, but see him, rather, as a creature to be gawped at rather as we might an animal at a zoo. Rameen knows better: 'Usama has made me more accepting of people who are different. It brings home to me that I wouldn't want to be stared at. We still get a lot of that – sometimes people stop and talk to each other and then they both turn to stare. We wouldn't mind if people asked – just *asked* us about Usama – but what we really don't want is people making us feel that there is something wrong with him.'

People who don't go so far as to stare at Usama may yet prefer to keep out of his parents' way, and when dropping off Usama at the school gates, Rameen noticed that 'parents would avoid me – quite a lot of them. I just learned to accept it.' But still she protests: 'Regardless of what you can do or achieve, you're still human. Usama just wants to be loved and happy.'

It is not that parents at the school gates believe that Usama is not a person; it is that some parents see Usama *as if* he is not. It is easily done, particularly if we don't know how to communicate with someone and find their gestures and expressions unfamiliar or off-putting. This does not apply to Kittay, mother of Sesha: 'We know there is a person before us when we see … that there is "someone home" … that the seemingly vacant look is not vacant at all':

> to be with Sesha is to enter her orbit, to gain a glimpse of the world as she constructs it … In one who can scarcely move a muscle, a glint in the eye at a strain of familiar music establishes personhood. A slight upturn of the lip in a profoundly and multiply disabled individual when a favourite caregiver comes along, or a look of joy in response to the scent of a perfume – all these establish personhood.
>
> *(2001: 568)*

Seeing Sesha's face as joyous means seeing it in human terms; viewing her gesticulation not as a muscular spasm or something indecipherable, but as an expressive act which reveals something about *Sesha*, and what she is seeking to communicate to others.

Clive Beecham is a teacher at Mayfield School. He too aims to read and interpret the children he has worked alongside for 16 years. His method of teaching emerged from working with children with PMLD and whose disabilities included deafness and blindness – the deaf/blind community: 'In my way of working I spend a lot of time just trying to get to know the kids. Knowing what the youngsters are using as their means of communication and learning how to respond to that.'

Clive showed me two videos of one of his pupils, 15-year-old Karim. In the first Karim is left to his own devices, and we see him sitting in his chair, with splints on his arms, making involuntary movements, his arms flailing, crying out angrily – almost roaring. In the second film, Clive is working with Karim, and he (Clive) is gently banging a drum whilst Karim is stilled, attentive and quiet. Karim is trying to control his arms in order to hold Clive's hand. One of Karim's arms is at rest, whilst he (Karim) is being held by Clive. For Clive 'this is all about learning from Karim – trying to make sense of how Karim is communicating and learning from that. We need to understand what his actions are actually trying to tell you. He has a right to be responded to, as I am trying to in the second film, and not ignored, as he is in the first. We have to make an effort to meet him halfway, so that we can learn from him and learn how to respond to him. This is an example of interaction using music, but it doesn't have to be music – it could be anything. The big thing is *let the child take the lead*, and we try to take them up on that and move on with something resembling a "conversation."'

Allowing the child to take the lead is to allow him a measure of control; but it is also a means of learning what the child most wants, and most wants to communicate. In this way, as Clive says, we can start a genuine conversation. It can take time and demand patience, but this is what is required by the injunction that we should treat human beings with respect, and with a willingness to see the world from their point of view.

5 Respect, recognition and the human point of view

I have held back from asking some awkward questions: is it always important that we make an effort to see another's point of view? Are the perspectives of people with profound disabilities always to be decisive in determining our behaviour and how we should think about them? What if those perspectives themselves give evidence of a lack of (self-) respect? Williams writes:

> [I]t is precisely a mark of extreme exploitation or degradation that those who suffer it do not see themselves differently from the way they are seen by the exploiters; either they do not see themselves as anything at all, or they acquiesce passively in the role for which they have been cast.
>
> *(1973: 237)*

Writers as diverse as Silvers and Goffman have described the rationalising and sometimes self-delusive strategies adopted by people whose subordination stems from disability or from the institutional demands to which disability renders them vulnerable (Silvers 1995; Goffman 1991). Pedagogy for learners with severe and complex learning difficulties emerged after psychologists working in long-stay hospitals found that institutionalised adults labelled as 'imbeciles', and considered unable to learn any social skills, could be trained to undertake numerous tasks for themselves (Mortimore 1999: 120). Those same adults, however, frequently constructed an image of themselves which selects from and distorts beliefs so as to arrive at a view that it is beneficial to expound in an institutional setting (Goffman 1991: 136–155). In other words, it is a characteristic of some people who are 'looked after', or who have become institutionalised, that their self-image embodies a lack of self-esteem and self-respect. In these cases we shouldn't always take their point of view as our lodestar for guiding our behaviour towards them; that would only serve to consolidate their subordination.

Of course, no one and no school featured in this book could be justly accused of oppressive or exploitative practices. On the contrary: the overriding aspiration is to develop human potential and to recognise someone for the person they either are or are capable of becoming. There would be whole-hearted agreement with Kittay when she writes:

> we do not become a person without the engagement of other persons – their care, as well as their recognition of the uniqueness and the connectedness of our human agency, and the distinctiveness of our particularly human relations in others and of the world we fashion.
>
> *(2001: 568)*

Engagement with others, on their own terms, can also provide the means and encouragement for personal development. For recognition by other humans contributes to a growing and stabilising sense of who we are and what we have the potential to become. There is suggestive evidence of this point from Watson and Fisher (1997), who examined the effectiveness of 'intensive interaction' teaching of pupils with profound and complex learning difficulties. Teachers respond to the learner's gestures, vocalisation, focus of attention and level of development, and they emphasise interaction between learner and teacher. The authors conclude:

> Levels of interest and motivation, the basis for all learning, were high … For pupils like these, often described as being totally dependent for all their needs, the importance of such experiences, which enable more meaningful involvement in their social world, cannot be overstated.
>
> *(Ibid: 86–87)*

This example of meticulous attentiveness illustrates how caring and teaching may come to be almost one and the same, as Corbett suggests, reflecting on her time as a teacher of young people with profound learning difficulties:

> What these young people taught me was that the communication which teaching involves includes careful listening and sensitive reciprocity … Teaching and caring were synonymous. I learnt to be careful, by which I mean to reflect on the way I communicated and responded. In this respect, it was about trying to treat vulnerable people with dignity. I see this as 'careful teaching', not separating the care from the teaching.
>
> *(1992: 237)*

The other end of the spectrum is represented by the denial of the validity or even the existence of someone's point of view. People who are systematically overlooked or mis-recognised by significant others or dominant groups are liable to be presented with a demeaning picture of themselves. Since identity is shaped by how we are recognised by others, this picture is likely to contribute to a confined sense of self and some erosion in the sense of our own worth (Taylor 1992). This explains why lack of respect is said by Frankfurt to imply the denial of a person and an assault on her reality:

> This sort of treatment … may naturally evoke painful feelings of resentment. It may also evoke a more or less inchoate anxiety; for when a person is treated as though significant elements of his life count for nothing, it is natural for him to experience this as in a certain way an assault upon his reality. What is at stake for him, when people act as though he is not what he is, is a kind of self-preservation. It is not his biological survival that is challenged, of course, when his nature is denied. It is the reality of his existence for others, and hence the solidity of his own sense that he is real.
>
> *(1999: 153)*

This is a powerful statement about the importance of respect, and goes some way to explaining why we are thought to have a basic duty to respect other persons, irrespective of their disability or any other distinguishing characteristic.

Yet there is a problem with the views expressed here. The need for acknowledgement or recognition is not universally acute, and not everyone will respond to lack of respect in the ways Frankfurt suggests. Whilst for some people their sense of reality may seem under threat, others may have a sufficiently robust sense of self to experience only the mildest resentment – if that – and certainly nothing approaching the existential crisis described above.

The point that different people respond differently to lack of respect applies to people with profound disabilities: not only because of their variable response to disrespectful behaviour, but also because some will remain largely unaware of what is withheld, and may not recognise 'lack of respect' under that description. Consider, then, how Veronica describes an incident with her daughter Harriet: 'I need to hold her dignity for her. I wanted only women handling her. I didn't want a male carer cleaning her nappy pads. Once Harriet ripped her clothes off and began to rip her nappy pads in a public space. Her carers formed a circle round her, and what they were doing was respecting her dignity. Of course, Harriet wouldn't understand these concepts, and couldn't protect her dignity herself. "Respect for dignity" is trying to understand the world from Harriet's perspective.'

It is important that we try to understand the world from Harriet's perspective, but this perspective may not help us determine what we should do in order to respect her dignity, since her perspective may not include any idea of respect, or dignity, and may not include any experience of behaviour that she understands in these terms.

Here, however, we should proceed with care. It might be thought that damage caused by disrespect will apply only to those who are capable of seeing themselves as having dignity and self-respect. But from the fact that a person does not make use of or understand such terms as 'dignity' and 'respect', it does not follow that she is not sensitive to behaviour that is more or less respectful, since this does not depend upon the ability to recognise oneself under these descriptions. Doubtless there are profoundly disabled people who do not conceive themselves as having dignity and as being owed respect. Yet by their behaviour and expressive repertoire they may provide evidence of growing or failing self-worth in response to how they are treated. This might be suggested, on the one hand, by a developing preparedness to experiment in a learning environment, and to engage with and learn from their peers; and, on the other hand, a tendency to withdraw from human contact and attempt less and less in the way of novel or even familiar learning activities (Fitton 1994; Norris 1982).

It is, in any case, often not easy to know how much people understand of what is said or what is going on around them. Lena Braun works with the children at Christ Church School whose levels of functioning and awareness are among the lowest that the school can work with. In response to the question whether these children would even notice features of behaviour that we might register as disrespectful, her response was forthright: 'We don't know!' And, because we don't know, we should assume that they understand more than we might imagine: 'How would anybody know that they hardly notice? You don't know exactly how much a child understands. So you have to assume that they do understand. Just because they can't tell you doesn't mean that they don't know this. We should assume that they know exactly what is going on. Although they can't show it, they might yet understand every word you're saying. They could be thinking all sorts of things, but they haven't got the voice to say it.'

Marjorie Clarke, Head at St Peter's, agrees: 'We don't talk over the heads of our children, or talk about them in front of them. We don't know what they can understand. Perhaps they do understand something, and perhaps they don't. My view is: *'just assume'* [that they understand]. One of the biggest dangers we face is failing to realise that a child is understanding something, or has the potential to understand.'

Lena and Marjorie are right to insist that, in general, we should assume that someone can understand enough for it to make a difference as to whether what is said and done to them is respectful or otherwise. Yet before we conclude this chapter we do have to confront cases in which any such understanding is (almost certainly) absent. Whilst as a general rule we can assume that human beings who are the object of respect have a point of view that other humans can engage with and respond to, not *all* profoundly disabled people will be capable of interaction of that order. If respect for a person is not to be abandoned if and when her cognitive faculties do not extend to recognising (dis)respectful words and actions, we are in need of reasons for respect that take *people* as their object, as distinct from the details of their cognitive lives.

One suggestion is that it matters less that a person should *actually* suffer from disrespect than that she is *entitled* to feel hurt when confronted with that attitude; the entitlement remains even if the feelings are absent. This is Raz's view:

> [W]e should respect people because we should not deny their reality. That duty may be more stringent when the people concerned are more liable to suffer from the hurt, but it is there whether or not they are actually likely to suffer.

(2002: 308)

Our duty to respect people with profound disabilities is related to their capacity to suffer, but we should also show respect for people regardless of their levels of suffering because we have a basic duty not to deny their reality. What is the basis of any such duty? One answer is that all people, including people with the profoundest disabilities, are human beings, and they are members of the same species as ourselves (Nozick 1997; Gaita 2000). Those who object to this view, however, suggest that it is 'speciesest' to assume that the moral status of any animal, human or otherwise, is related to the species they belong to; rather, what we should take account of are all but only the characteristics that are intrinsic to any one individual (Rachels 1986; McMahan 2002).

I cannot consider these arguments here. Rather, it is appropriate to end with some words from Daniel, a teacher at St Peter's School, whose thoughts are echoed by many who live and work in the world of profound disability. For Daniel there is no question but that all the children he works with have a human dignity and should be accorded a basic respect. Even a child like Sam, introduced previously, and who is functioning at very low levels, can and should be treated with dignity. What does this mean? For Daniel it means ensuring that all Sam's needs are met, that he is not abused in any way, and that no one is taking any liberties with him just because he can't stand up for himself. I began an earlier sentence with the words '*even* a child like Sam', but Daniel, I am sure, would have replaced 'even' with '*especially*': 'Sam should be treated with respect *because everyone should be treated with respect*. He's unlike you and me but he's still a human being. He is so different and can't look after himself – but that's why he deserves all the protection that goes with respecting someone.'

Some people can't look after themselves and that is a reason for providing them with the support and protection they need. But for Daniel we owe them this much, and more, anyway: for they are human beings and our fellow creatures, and that is reason enough to treat them with respect, and to maintain as a guiding aim the preservation of their dignity in everything that we do.

6 Concluding remarks

Respect for the human dignity of every human being is a precept that features prominently in many of the world's most influential declarations of human rights. The very first article, Article 1, of the Universal Declaration of Human Rights (UDHR), declares: 'All human beings are born free and equal in dignity and rights' (United National General Assembly 1948). In this chapter we have explored how dignity and respect apply to people with profound disabilities: what it means, in practice, to respect the dignity of people who may themselves have very little idea of what dignity means, and what respect requires.

A striking feature of much of the testimony presented here is how some people will simply treat a person with profound disabilities in the same way as they would treat anyone else. Of course almost everything they do and say is inflected by sensitivity to profound disability; but that is consistent with treating someone, in a very basic sense, just as they would treat you or me. If we choose to listen to Daniel, Leonda, Sian, Lena, Rameen or Marjorie: you do not talk over someone's head; you do not stare at someone; you do not pull their wheelchair backwards; and you do not leave the toilet door open when toileting. And you do not do these things to people even if they may not understand what you are doing or why you are doing it. Above all, you do not do these things because every human being, irrespective of their impairments, no matter how many or how profound, has a basic human dignity that we should all of us recognise and respect. It is inspiring to witness care and teaching infused with these convictions, and they are in the spirit of the opening words of the UDHR: 'Whereas recognition of the inherent dignity and of the equal and inalienable rights of all members of the human family is the foundation of freedom, justice and peace in the world' (United Nations General Assembly 1948).

Points for discussion

- Do all human beings have dignity?
- Are all human beings owed respect?
- Is human dignity intrinsic to human beings, or, rather, accorded to them in virtue of how they are seen and treated by others?
- Should it make any difference to how we should treat someone whether or not they understand what we are doing?
- 'What you don't know can't hurt you': why should we not talk over a child's head if he is quite oblivious to what we are doing?

8

CARING FOR PROFOUNDLY DISABLED PEOPLE

In practice

1 Introduction

This chapter is unlike any of the others in that its principal purpose is simply to let carers speak for themselves; they offer eloquent and vivid accounts of what it is like to live with and care for a child who is profoundly dependent. Carers of children with profound learning disabilities will be familiar with a lot of what is written here. But they often remark that other parents, and other people generally, must have little idea of what their lives are like. Parent-carers might overhear parents of mainstream children complaining about the volume of homework, and the likely reaction is: 'How little they know! If only that were the limit of what I had to cope with!' This chapter should give some idea of the demands and routines that fill the lives of carers with profoundly disabled children.

The demands on carers differ one to another, and each day in the life of each carer is different. Living in a one bedroom flat with a family of five is a world apart from living in a three bedroom house with a family of four. A day which includes a violent seizure brings demands that are additional to those that characterise a day without complications. And if a child is in good health, then his carers' lives will be very different to those who care for children whose health is precarious or deteriorating.

Even so, it is worth recording the experiences of a handful of carers. Although each of their stories is unique, each includes many features that characterise the lives of people who care for highly dependent children: the routines and arrangements, demands and impositions, anxieties and frustrations, the tiredness and 'never-endingness' of care – along with the surprises, satisfactions, rewards and joys.

The chapter is divided into two parts: in section 2 we hear from Heather, who describes her two profoundly disabled grandchildren and takes us through 24 hours in her life as their primary carer; whilst section 3 presents the experience of several parent-carers, and illustrates some of the many facets of caring for profoundly disabled people.

2 A day and night in the life of Heather Peterson

Heather, Isla and Patrick

Heather Peterson is a white British 57-year-old grandmother, who has three children and five grandchildren. Two of her grandchildren have multiple and profound learning difficulties: Patrick, the eldest, who is 16 and in palliative care; and his half sister, Isla, who is 7, and who attends a special school for children with profound learning difficulties.

Heather cares (on her own) for Patrick and Isla, after her daughter was no longer able to look after the children by herself. 'In a previous life I was a designer working in the fashion and home furnishing industry and I taught part time in Higher Education.' But her life was to change. 'My daughter has mental health problems. When Patrick was 5 she became unable to cope. I respect the fact that she was absolutely determined that Patrick was placed safely before she became too ill.'

After Patrick came to Heather she managed to work for a while but as his health deteriorated it became obvious that she needed to be at home full time. 'Then Isla came to me when she was 9 months old and I've been at home since looking after both children. It was a huge change in my life and I must admit that in the beginning I wondered how on earth things would turn out. But I never regret the decision. I feel that this is absolutely what I should be doing at this time, particularly since Patrick won't be here forever. I would hate to miss this time.'

How would Heather describe Isla? 'She's a very happy child, loves swimming, happily potters about, very tactile and loving, loves kisses and cuddles.' Isla responds best to adults: 'She is quite happy to play alongside her cousins and other children, but she doesn't interact a great deal. She is very sensitive to noise and she covers her ears a lot if sound becomes too difficult for her to cope with. She is sometimes very energetic, and sometimes she just likes to snuggle under a blanket. She doesn't have a diagnosis beyond "global developmental delay", although we know that she has multi-focal epilepsy. She is mobile at the moment, but her ability to walk is becoming more affected as her epilepsy changes. She has no speech and her vocalisation is very limited and depends on how well she is feeling. Everything depends on the state of her epilepsy.'

'Isla has a gastrostomy and is tube fed as a result of having an impaired swallow. She is doubly incontinent and wears nappies. She has sight and hearing, although her hearing as I mentioned is very sensitive. She doesn't use vision as her first point of reference. For instance, she doesn't recognise changes in levels – so stairs for example, are dangerous. She uses sound and touch as her first senses. She has absolutely no sense of danger and seems to seek out strong sensory input. So, she'll trap her fingers in a drawer or put her face on a hot radiator, or walk straight off the top stair. She needs constant care to keep her safe.'

And Patrick? 'Patrick has no diagnosis beyond "global developmental delay" and "multi-focal, polymorphic epilepsy", which means that his seizures emanate from many parts of the brain and that they are ever changing and never completely under control. We know at least that he has a deteriorating condition – since being small his health problems have changed and increased. He has developed scoliosis [curvature of the spine] which is so severe that without the help of strong drugs his pain would be severe and constant. He has a gastrostomy and is tube fed, he has no speech, and no gross or fine motor skills. He is visually impaired: when he was younger and still mobile the doctors established that although he had sight, it was confused and he didn't have any sense of what was near or far – he judged something by its size. Patrick has a compromised respiratory system, and he has a pseudomonas infection – a bacterial infection which colonises in his lungs. He suffers from recurring chest infections and requires 24-hour oxygen to help him breathe. Patrick also has a distonic movement disorder which is very tiring for him. He requires 1:1 care at the very least.'

'Patrick is receiving palliative care only. We have decided that it would be unfair to intervene with any further aggressive treatment – that is, no intravenous antibiotics and no more intensive care. His condition is so poor already and is worsening. It would be unkind to endlessly prolong his life. He's very tired at every part of the day. He's dealing with a lot of pain and has to take an enormous amount of medication. He's now at the point where he is unable to pass urine or stools without help. Everything is coming to a halt – things are breaking down. He's sedated for quite a lot of the time. He really has quite a difficult time. He was much like Isla when he was younger – mobile and able to enjoy things in life, and I have seen that slowly change over the years. I see similarities in their conditions, and I'm afraid that the signs are that Isla may follow the same path as Patrick.'

A typical 24 hours

What is a typical day and night in the life of Heather Peterson? Much of it is taken up with cleaning, ordering, monitoring, managing stocks of medications, and liaising with doctors and pharmacists. There is the daily cleaning and checking of equipment, including oxygen cylinders and concentrators, the nebuliser, masks and tubing, the suction machine, suction catheters, tubing and chambers. 'I need to be monitoring and informing medical teams of changes in the children's conditions and fitting in appointments, both at home and at hospitals; and I need to coordinate carers and their shifts. And last but not least – we do the usual family stuff, have friends to dinner and socialise … very important!'

'My day begins at 4.30am or so, depending on whether Patrick is unsettled. On the best days (these are rare) I would wake at 6am. My first job, after making sure that Patrick is comfortable, is to pull up all of the children's medications. Then, during term time, Jean, one of my carers, will come to work between 7 and 8.30am. Jean will give Patrick his medication (around 15 syringes) whilst I prepare their feeds – both children are tube fed. I prepare Patrick's milk feed and Isla's breakfast feed. Then I get the clean clothes and nappies for both children. Next I run Patrick's bath whilst Jean undresses him. We hoist Patrick into the bath and I wash him, brush his teeth and wash his hair. We hoist him out of the bath, wrap him in warm towels and then Jean will dress Patrick whilst I get Isla up and bathed and dressed. I attend to her stoma which needs dressing each day and then give her her medications (usually five syringes) and her breakfast feed. Then I prepare Isla's lunch and feeds for the day to take to school, make sure that the feeding tube is clean and that there is a sufficient supply of syringes, and make sure the daily home-school diary is written up accurately so that the school know what sort of night Isla has had.'

'Jean leaves for work at 8.30 (she works at the school Isla attends). If she has time before she leaves she will put Patrick's feed on and a nebuliser. If not then I do, having first cleaned the masks, making sure that the tubing is OK. Then I get Isla's coat, hat and gloves on, put her into her wheelchair, pack her school bag with anything she needs and wait for the school bus to arrive to take her to school. Once the bus arrives at the door I take her out to put her on the bus.'

'Then my day begins with Patrick. I prepare his antibiotic nebuliser and make sure he is comfortable. He is usually quite settled by 9.30 after morning medication so I am then able to make the beds, put the next load of washing in, change Isla's bed (which happens every day), and do whatever housework needs to be done, though I am constantly checking that Patrick is OK. If he needs help then the housework has to wait. From that point my day is totally dependent upon Patrick's needs. If he has a chest infection he will have a nebuliser every hour; if not then this is a little less frequent. He requires suctioning throughout the day to clear secretions. He needs to be catheterised at several points during the day to help him pass urine, and two or three times a week he will need an enema to help him to open his bowels.'

'Because Patrick accesses the world on a purely sensory level I like to provide as much input as possible. I like to put music on for him and have some sort of sensory lighting, perhaps one of the laser lights projected onto the ceiling so that if he wakes he will have something lovely to see. Maybe dangle some light or reflective toys from his hoist so that they reach his hands, something tactile. I give him plenty of hand and foot massages to relax him, and so that he is aware of his extremities. I also give him something lovely to smell. I read to him a lot, he loves that.'

'This takes us to lunchtime. Time to prepare his afternoon medications. I usually leave some music playing or an audio book. The choice is anything from classical to Led Zeppelin to Rhianna or Amy Winehouse – just so that he hears a variation. I try to keep things age appropriate. It would be very easy to just put on a Disney film and forget that, actually, he's a 16-year-old boy and probably sick to the back teeth of Disney!'

'Patrick will rest for most of the day, though he will have bouts of movement disorder, need his chest clearing and have seizures. He needs regular changes of position to help with pain and chest congestion and so that he doesn't get stiff or uncomfortable, and of course he needs regular feeds. Patrick takes his feeds over a three or four hour period – any faster and it becomes difficult for him to deal with. The times in between are the times when I will grab a bite to eat.'

'We have a "tiger room" – a room next to the living room. It's a soft room where we have cushions and a large padded area – it's where we keep lots of sensory stuff, all of the toys and the TV and DVDs. We sometimes all pile into the tiger room!'

'The afternoons tend to follow a similar pattern, though I have to check whether we need repeat prescriptions, or order nappies, make appointments and the like. I need to get ready for Isla returning from school at 3.30pm. I have a carer – one of my NHS Continuing Care 'dream' Team for children with complex and life-limiting conditions – between 3.30pm and 7 or 8pm, depending upon the hours available. I will prepare a bottle and feed for Isla, which she tends to have in the tiger room. She loves to relax there after school. If the weather is good we might go for a walk or play on the swing or trampoline in the garden if she's well enough. I'm very concerned that she has play time – the stuff that other children have.'

'I prepare dinner for the carer and myself, we pull up all the evening medications, get Isla washed and changed into her pyjamas and I give her her medication. Big cuddles, maybe a story and then it's up to bed for Isla at around 7.30pm. Then we have our dinner. Patrick has his medications shortly afterwards and is ready for bed at around 8.30–9pm.'

'Of course if Isla is unwell and at home rather than at school, or if her seizures are too difficult for her – then I have both children at home and I care for both of them on my own. Often, when Isla has lots of seizures, she vomits, poor thing, so there's lots of cleaning up to be done. There are often times when it all "kicks off" at the same time and they will both have seizures, or Patrick will have a bout of movement and Isla will be sick – these are the times when it can get difficult.'

'On Wednesday afternoons I attend a "music and movement" group with Isla at school between 1pm and 2.45pm, so I have a carer for Patrick from the Continuing Care Team. The carer comes from 10am until 6pm, and that gives me the opportunity to do a little shopping or anything that needs to be done outside home.'

'Because of Patrick's oxygen needs, his suction requirements and his need for nebulisers, and of course his seizures, his care management doesn't stop at night. Isla often has seizures at night too, so it's not unusual to be up and down stairs between Patrick and Isla for most of the night. I stay downstairs with Patrick – his bedroom is on the ground floor. I don't really get much sleep – I snooze, but don't really sleep soundly. Because his swallowing is impaired and is not really effective it's important to keep his airways clear by suctioning. Isla has her bedroom upstairs. I have a baby alarm in Isla's room, so that if she has a seizure or needs help I can hear her and run upstairs. On the nights that I'm alone (four in every seven) I might be able to snooze for two to four hours.'

'And then it all begins again … But what I have been describing is a school day. During the weekends and holidays I get the children up and ready for the day and put them to bed at night on my own. By doing so I can make the best use of the Direct Payment hours. It's best to have someone with me between 10 and 6pm – it means we can make the most of the day.'

Heather could hardly do more for her grandchildren, but she cannot do everything. 'It's quite a difficult thing to come to terms with – that you can't offer everything to the children, all of the time, unaided. It would mean that I would "burn out" and I have to be mindful of the children's needs first and foremost. I must say that I have a terrific team around Patrick and Isla – largely from the NHS

Continuing Care Team. They supply a healthcare assistant to be with Patrick, usually for three overnight shifts per week. The carers know Patrick very well and I can trust them; if and when there are any problems they wake me. It means that I can go to bed, though I do still get up throughout the night to care for Isla.'

The presence of support can make the difference between getting a good night's sleep and not: 'We have just had another assessment and I may be able to have a carer for Isla one night per week if the decision goes in our favour. That would mean one night per week that I could sleep!'

In addition to support from the Continuing Care Team, Heather receives 'Direct Payment' hours from Social Services – 25 hours per week for Patrick and 18 hours a week for Isla. 'This means that I am able to employ carers to help me care for the children. I put Patrick's and Isla's hours together, and work out the "hotspots" so that I have help at the busiest times. I have four carers who work the Direct Payment hours; all of them are employed at the school that Isla attends (and which Patrick previously attended). They are all trained in epilepsy and manual handling, and have known Patrick and Isla for many years.'

I ask Heather what keeps her going: 'My grandchildren keep me going! Their needs keep me going; the necessity to put things right as much as I can – because they absolutely deserve it.'

3 The experience of parent-carers

Heather's testimony provides a snapshot of a day and night in the life of one carer. We now hear from five mothers, each of whom brings out some of the distinctive aspects of caring for and living with children with profound disabilities.

Jo, Dean, Alex and Rowena

I first introduced Jo in Chapter 2, in a discussion of toileting and sexuality. Jo is 42, white British, and married to Dean, who is 45. 'Lovely!', she says of Dean. 'I'm very, very lucky!' Her elder child, Rowena, is 17. She's a 'clever girl – As and Bs in her GCSEs. She's now in the sixth form and wants to do religious studies – we are a religious family.'

Her younger child is Alex. Alex is 14 and is diagnosed as having medium functioning autism, global developmental delay and as being hyperactive. 'He is definitely severely disabled – maybe severe, maybe profound. He'll never live independently. Physically he's fine: he walks, runs, jumps, dances. He can walk unassisted, though I might have to follow him to make sure he goes where I want him to go. Alex is funny, loving. *Now* he's loving. He wasn't loving when he was younger – he wasn't able to show affection. Now he will ask for cuddles as well as happily receive them. He is caring. He does care for me. If I was crying he would wipe my eyes – even if he might accidentally poke my eyes out at the same time! He is aware of other people's emotions – slightly. It's difficult: there is definitely a person under the disability – and a personality. But the disability has a major impact on the personality. Because Alex is functioning at the toddler level. He's helpful and he's beginning to be helpful without being asked. He's just a cheeky, loving young man.'

The family as a team

'I've been married 21 years. I'm so lucky. Dean took a long, long time to accept Alex. He buried his head in the sand. Dean doesn't do emotions. He's very clever. But now we're on to it. We're together as a team. Now, if I go away for the weekend, Dean will manage. I can't even write a cheque – I'm dyslexic. Dean does all of that. But I am better with Alex. We have an old-fashioned marriage. Because I'm dyslexic Dean does all the paperwork and I do all the cleaning. But one thing our house is full of is *laughter and love*.'

'And Rowena is the most amazing sister. She completely loves her brother, and never, ever resented him, always interacting with him. She's become more mature, being with Alex. She wants to be a minister. Who do you know who at 17 wants to be a minister? She says "I have a good brain and I want to use it."'

Alex then and now

How was it caring for Alex when he was younger? 'Horrific! Alex was a *nightmare* when he was young! He would climb everywhere, smear poo, turn the gas on. He was in a major [large] buggy then. He had no language, wouldn't sleep, up all night. And that was from about one and a half to four. And then things started to get better and now we have very little of all that. Very few wobblies – though, whenever we get one, it looks worse than it is because he is so big.'

'He's gone beyond our expectations. *We are so proud of him* – he's done his very best to be a good boy. Every now and then he loses it … but so do we all.'

Complex feelings

'I am *not* one of those amazing parents who would say: "I wouldn't want my child any other way." Because I would. If I could sell everything I own to make Alex normal I would do it in an instant. I feel bad that I am not one of those amazing parents. But I'm honest. It would make everyone's life better – including Alex's life. It's not a selfish thing – it's for all of us. But I love him for the person he is. I do feel waves of guilt when I meet parents with more difficulties than Alex, and they say, "I wouldn't have it any other way."'

'Do I love Alex and Rowena equally? I used to have a dream. Our house was on fire. I didn't stand in the hallway deliberating. I got Rowena first. Then, in my dream, I think, "Do I go back and get Alex?" Then I would wake up from the dream and my first feeling was one of relief, because now we would have a normal life. But then, immediately, I would feel guilt. When I spoke to the psychiatrist about the dream he would say, "You're practical; you want what is best for you from a practical point of view." I used to have this dream when Alex was younger and things were more difficult.'

'I love both my children, but Alex needs more love, takes more love and tests my love more. He needs constantly to be taking from you.'

'I'm a good mum to both of my children. I do it because I have no choice. If I had a choice Alex wouldn't be here. If they had told me in the womb Alex will be autistic, Alex wouldn't be here. I would not have chosen to make my life this hard. It's the constant fighting. *Having no time for me.* You almost become an extension of Alex. It's all about Alex, Alex, Alex. You're up all night, no sleep, you're shot to bits, you're legs are shaking and you just feel absolutely horrendous. And then you feel selfish, for thinking "What about me?" Because your child's needs should always come first.'

'What is most difficult? Knowing that *you will never, ever have a normal life and there is not a damned thing you can do about it.* And people will pity you, and I don't like that. It can take a long time to adapt. Dean adapted better than me to how things are. I'd say, "Alex is 14 – he could be out there playing football." And Dean would say, "That's irrelevant! Alex is not like that, that's a stupid thing to say."'

A right to a home

'The hardest thing is that we wanted Alex in a home when he was 19. And now we've been told that that would take a miracle. I'm *praying* for a miracle! I've worked *so hard* to make Alex the boy he is. One day I will die. I need to know he will be safely looked after. I've strived – *really, really worked* – to make him independent. And *no one* – not the government, the council – has the right not to give Alex a place that is right for him. That's the *scariest* thing. I could be old and grey and I may never have or enjoy my retirement with Dean, my hubby. We could almost be being penalised for doing so well with Alex. I think Alex has a right to a home with other people at the same level, with experienced staff, 24-hour supervision, and with support that will help Alex to have the most independence he can have, and a happy life.'

'But there's very little chance of a home – verging on no chance. When I heard this I cried for several hours. And then I thought to myself, "It's no good crying, take it day by day, and worry about that when it comes." Who knows, we could win the lottery and go private. Alex deserves as much as any other child. Perhaps more. Because he has more needs. And he has no voice. I am his voice, and he's very lucky to have a trained mum. [Jo works in the school that Alex attends.] He should be respected as much as anyone.'

How others react

'Sometimes it's how people react that gets to you. When Alex was younger he had a temper tantrum in a supermarket, and he hit someone, and she was very, very abusive. Now he's a placid young man, but still children will ask, "What's wrong with Alex?'' and I see the mums pulling the children away as if their children are going to catch something. And that is really, really awful.'

Love

'You can tell, he absolutely loves me, just as I absolutely love him. I am the main person in his world. He doesn't just love me. He needs me. He can give me happiness. Like, for example, last night he came home with his woodwork. And it was really rubbish! But we really loved it! And just seeing him growing, developing and being the best person he can possibly be, which is the same goal as Rowena has.'

Krystyna, Dmitri and James

Krystyna, who made a brief appearance in Chapters 2 and 5, is 28 and Polish, and her partner, Dmitri, 32, is Greek. They have lived in England for 10 and 15 years respectively. Both Krystyna and Dmitri work. Krystyna has her own business, providing catering facilities on building sites. She is a strong, proud, loving mother, and gives the impression that nothing is too much. Her son James is 5. 'James, he is a special boy – for me, his father, my parents; special for everybody. He has epilepsy, poor vision, seizures in the brain, and global developmental delay. He has no diagnosis beyond that. He can see bright light, and I think he has some sight – the problem is that he can't process what he sees. He can hear very well – and this compensates for his poor sight. He doesn't touch by himself and he doesn't hold any toys. He doesn't hold his head, and he can't sit on his own – he will flop back. He can't crawl, he can't walk. He has no language, but he can vocalise. I understand him well, but *not* from his talking, but from how he reacts and behaves. And James understands me – from the voice, the touch, the kisses. I have a good understanding with him.'

'He's a happy boy. When he's feeling well he's a really happy boy. He's laughing, smiling, pushing his legs, vocalising a lot – very bubbly. When he's happy he has *lots* of energy. He will sometimes go 48 hours without sleep – that tends to happen once a week. If he doesn't have his jerks [his seizures], then he's happy. When he wakes up in the morning – and even when he wakes at night – then he's smiling – never crying.'

The first years

'When James was born everyone was happy – he looked like a normal boy. We didn't think that anything was wrong for at least a year. It was only when my mum started to notice that his eye contact was not good – that he didn't look at your eyes when you walked into the room. We went to the GP, and he said that everything will be fine: "Some kids will develop late." I was a young mum and I thought that the GP must be right. But later my mum said, "Something is really wrong with James." So we went to a neurologist at Great Ormond Street, and he was given lots of tests. They realised that he was having seizures in the brain. We were shocked and depressed. "Why us? What have we done wrong? Why? Why? Maybe we can help him." I went back to Poland to get other opinions from GPs there but they couldn't help. And James continued to have tests, including genetic tests, but we were told that his genes were OK. Again, the results from this test showed nothing amiss. The doctors said to us: "Sometimes we come across children and we can't find out what is wrong with them". James was then about two to two and a half. We tried loads of medications but he was reacting adversely to these. So we decided, over the last two years, not to give James any of these medications because it wasn't helping him.'

This is my life – I just have to live with it

'My life back then? My life was really hard. It was hard to realise that I had a boy like this. But then, you start to realise that this is your life and you just have to live with it. Now, it's less emotionally taxing and more physically difficult – he's getting heavier. Before, it was hard to take James out with other children who were normal – because you can see … it's kind of embarrassing – they are watching you. You feel bad when you see other children running around and calling out "Mum!" – and you think, "I wish my boy could do this." It takes a lot of time to adjust, to get to the stage when you can say, "This is my life, I just have to live with it."'

'Emotionally, I feel much better than before. You still think, "Maybe I can help him." I try to do the very best for him. *Little steps. Step by step.* We won't ever have a healthy child. But when he makes a small step it's a miracle for us. And it is not as painful now as it was. And it's easier for me because my whole family is here – my mum, my father, and my grandfather. They all support me. If it wasn't for them I *definitely* couldn't cope on my own. And I get loads of support from my friends – I couldn't cope without all the support I get.'

Not knowing what's wrong

'Sometimes, when he's not happy, it's hard to tell what exactly is wrong with him. That is hard. And one of the other hardest things is not being able to help. Early on, when doctors were trying to find out what was wrong, they needed to take liquid from his spine. It was so hard to hold my boy whilst he was in pain as the liquid was taken. The nurse said that I should leave, but I couldn't leave my boy. He was looking into my eyes as if to say, "Mummy – help me."'

Tiredness and loneliness

'What is most difficult is when he's not sleeping – sometimes not for 48 hours – and you get just 5–10 minutes sleep, and you become emotionally tired and upset. Then emotionally you sometimes feel *just so tired*, and then I might shout at James. But then you feel so bad – you know that James can't change – he can't help it. Or, even when he's crying you just feel so bad – you don't always know how to help him. Or I get a call from the school – "Why is James crying?" – and I don't always know. Or, say that you want to go on holiday together, all three of us, and we can't go. Because it's hard with the food, for example – you need to feed him every three hours, and he doesn't cope with the heat.'

'Even my close family, sometimes you think, "You understand, but *you don't understand how I feel*." Sometimes, I think, even with Dmitri, "*You don't understand just how tired I am*." And of course when you are so tired, you get upset, you have arguments with your partner. Tiredness is the hardest thing – I'm always tired.'

'Sometimes, for half the night it's Dmitri who is holding James's hand – James wants his hand held – and half the night I do this. If we leave him in his bed alone then he will wake up. For a short time, now, I'm not working – for two to three months – so it's me who is with James all night. The good thing is that James is now at school, and so I can get one or two hours of sleep during the day.'

'I spend most of the day with James. And sometimes it's *lonely* – being on my own.'

I always want more

'Dmitri says, "This is our life, there's nothing we can do, nothing we can change, we have to take what we have." But me, I always have hope inside my heart, that I can still help him, do something to help him. Probably, I will never accept that there is nothing I can do anymore. I will always try to do the very best for my boy.'

Sally, Andrew, Paul and Ewan

The 'lioness'

Sally is the 50-year-old mother of two children, Ewan, 21, and Paul, who is 17 and whose multiple and profound learning difficulties include autism spectrum disorder. Her husband, Andrew, is 54. Sally describes herself as a 'lioness', and that is how she comes across. 'Often, when I'm walking with Paul in public he will make a certain movement – it's a bit like a hop, skip and a flap – his hands will flap – and he makes a sound that is a bit like a roar. He's tall, and people will watch and look at him and see this big, peculiar man. A lot of it is ignorance. If it's a child staring you can understand. But if it's an adult I will humiliate them. I will make them feel embarrassed and ashamed if they just stare and nudge each other. If they dare laugh I'll give them a piece of my mind.'

'I'll give you an example. We were in Turkey, Paul, me and Andrew, in 2011. Everywhere we went, people stared – they literally did this in front of our faces. They would look at Paul and nudge each other. One day, we were sitting by our pool. Everyone was looking at Paul, and they were giggling and snickering. When he walked towards the pool's edge the men were looking at him, laughing at him openly. They didn't see me. I stomped up to them and said, "How *dare* you! Can you not see that something is wrong with my son?" That's what gave me strength, actually – like being the lioness, if you like.'

What Paul gives to Sally

'When we were in Turkey a lot of other things happened. We were three days into the holiday and my husband, Andrew, had a thoracic aortic aneurysm. He was given a 30 per cent chance of survival. So I had my husband and my child to worry about! We stayed in Turkey for a month whilst my husband recovered. If it wasn't for Paul, I would have had a nervous breakdown. It was the hardest time of my life and Paul helped me. I had to get out of the hotel to help Paul at night. We used to look for an internet café – I had to entertain my son. I had to focus on Paul, enjoying himself, bless him, enjoying himself as much as he can. He helped me. I had to focus on him. I would have gone under, had a nervous breakdown, if it wasn't for him. Paul helped me through it without even realising it – bless him! – by just being himself, just being Paul.'

'I can't imagine being without him. He's very affectionate. He's very loving. If he sees me cry, he can't handle it. He can't bear to see me upset. He's enriched our lives so much. And, of course, *of course*, he matters as much to me as Ewan does. They matter exactly the same. I wouldn't even buy a sweet for one and not the other.'

'The most precious thing is him – his love. That's why I'm still in this school. To find out as much as I can, to help him when he leaves. It's all for him. All for him. A lot of parents don't know about funding, schools … I've got to find out for myself for Paul. I have to know that whatever his next step is that it's the best one.'

We never go out

'You cannot have a normal life. We never go out as husband and wife. Paul wouldn't stay with anyone else. What people take for granted, like going out as a couple, we can't do. If we ever go somewhere new, I would have to give Paul a "countdown", keep on reminding him, it's now two weeks away, one week away. He wouldn't like it, but when the time came, he would accept it. But you couldn't do anything quickly.'

What happens after I'm gone?

'I gave up smoking for Paul. I thought, "I need to live as long as I possibly can – I'm not going to smoke and encourage anything." I've never gone back. I need to live for him, as long as I can. I want him to be OK and happy. I want him to live as happy a life as anyone. I want him to be looked after – he'll never be independent. If I think about his long-term future I'd have a nervous breakdown. This is what is most difficult – worrying about Paul's future. I take each year as it comes. My first battle is – what is going to happen after here, after this school? I want Paul to progress, to be the man he is going to want to be.'

'I think the government has a responsibility to look after him. I'm not asking for 24-hour care – I'm just asking the government to provide funding so that he can be as independent as he can.'

'School. Education. *As long as Paul is learning* – that's the way for him. That's what makes him tick, that's what makes him happy.'

Jamila, Ade and Omari

Jamila Ademola is a single mother of two boys, Ade and Omari. Jamila is an Asian Muslim, and was born in Uganda in 1972. Ade is 20 and lives at home. He is diagnosed as having global developmental delay, severe difficulties with communication, and has to be looked after at all times. He is tall – 6 foot 2 inches.

'Ade is very friendly, loving, always smiling, happy. At home he's happy. Whoever comes into the house he will shake their hand, regardless of who you are. The college he attends – he will shake hands with the students in his class – he will shake their hands even if they feel uneasy. And he's very clever: when I'm out of the room he will start making his vocal sounds but when I'm in the room he's quiet. He has no language – he vocalises, makes sounds. He has good vision and hearing, and now he can sit and walk without assistance. He can't dress himself – unless you give him all his clothes in the right order. When he goes to the toilet I need to clean him.'

'He's very helpful at dinner. He brings the plates and puts them out, and later brings them back and puts everything away. I don't feed him. But if the dinner is ready on the table he won't feed himself; he will wait for me to put food on his plate.'

'Ade is a vulnerable child – he really is vulnerable. Once he had a new carer, and he didn't ask any questions, he just went off with her. He could be led anywhere. Crossing roads – he won't look, he will just cross over. He would be vulnerable to being mistreated by people. And the only way he will let you know anything is wrong is through his body language – he won't let you know in any other way.'

'His brother Omari loves Ade and Ade loves Omari. Omari knows that it is his responsibility to look after his brother, and he accepts that. Out of his own choice he gives Ade a shower, he grooms him – Ade has a beard – and he takes Ade to the hairdresser and goes out for walks with him.'

'Ade loves gardening. He wears his overall, sweeps the leaves, never gets tired. He's a child who is very physical, doing, rather than sitting and writing. At the Centre he goes to they grow their own vegetables, and sell them in a little store. I'd love to see him sitting somewhere doing a job like this. I wouldn't like to put him in a residential home when I pass away. And Omari would like to look after him, even if the person he marries is not happy with that!'

'What I would most want for Ade is that he come out of his autism. I've been told, "He is happy to be in his world." But it would be good if we had been able to get him out of that world. He deserves to have a good life, like everyone else. In the world he should live in he would be very safe, and he'd be working, looking after himself. One parent said to me: "The ideal place for our children would be an island somewhere, which is so safe that they can do what they want, where they aren't threatened or alarmed by anyone."'

Violence

'With my [former] partner, Ade saw a lot of violence towards me. I don't know if my partner would ever have been violent towards Ade – I don't know. Ade was very frightened of him. My partner was strict, and I was not strict; he left when Ade was 7. Ade witnessed a lot of things, a lot of violence. He doesn't like shouting and screaming and he saw a lot of this. The violence and the shouting affected him. At two he was able to speak a few words and then he just stopped, and this coincided with the violence. I just had to blank out the violence and the abuse. I don't think it had anything to do with Ade; it was to do with me – my partner just didn't like me or accept me. And I just had to get on with life; I had to. I just accepted that my partner was like that.'

Racism

'My neighbourhood is not very good. The other kids didn't understand autism. Because Ade makes noises the kids throw things – bricks even – into our garden when we are there. Kids used to chuck things and break the windows. When Ade was young he stood close to the window. He was very lucky. One boy threw a stone, breaking the window, and Ade was very lucky not to be hurt.'

'It used to be white people. Now black people have moved in and they abuse Ade through the walls – they call him all sorts of names and Ade has to get through that even though he doesn't speak, he doesn't understand. I think they just don't like Asian people; they abuse Ade, banging on the walls, shouting names, not letting us sleep. The banging on the walls used to go on to 2am or 3am. Because Ade couldn't speak he used to laugh. But now he will look at me, and I will see that seriousness – that he has heard his name being called, and he looks not frightened but upset. This is the third year of this. I'm not frightened of them. I tried to reason with them. But it just went worse. They didn't want me to talk to them. So every day they bang on the walls. They swear. I'm just baffled why they are doing it. We're the only Asian family on the street – but we're staying.'

'Why don't I move? Well, if I move from this area to another what if it was worse there? You can't keep running away. You have to stand your ground sometimes. All the time! If I show weakness my elder son will show weakness as well. There is no more stone throwing now; just the banging and the name calling.'

Jennifer and David

Jennifer is a former GP and obstetrician. She has three children, including David, aged 10, who has profound and multiple learning difficulties and disabilities. Jennifer says of David that 'he seems to be able to inspire so much goodwill in people – he inspires people to be good. It's nice to see the good in human nature being drawn out by David – I love that about David.' And family is everything: 'The most important thing is working together as a family. We've all learned to sacrifice time on our own. We've all learned to value time together as a family. We've learned to slow down. To have more time for each other – not to be so busy – both children and parents.'

Status and 'work–life' balance

'It was very difficult to work, to carry on with my job. I'm now a pathologist. I moved away from Obstetrics and Gynaecology because I didn't want to work shifts and weekends. I was halfway through to qualifying as a consultant and then decided that I needed to change and start again. I just couldn't do a nine to five – it was too exhausting and I think it probably had an adverse psychological impact.'

'You have a view of your status – I worked hard at school, went to a good university, I was ready for a good job. And I had a sense of having all my expectations turned on themselves. It's the whole career thing – that's the main thing. I could do it if I spent most of my wages on someone to care for David, but it's the tight emotional bond that you want to preserve. It's just there; it's just a given. There is just an immense amount of difficulty in sorting out the right people to look after him. It's the work–life balance – it's difficult for anyone but even more exhausting if you have a disabled child.'

Tiredness, exhaustion and the 'forever' factor

'For me, to be his mum, it's emotionally difficult – especially when communication breaks down. If he's screaming and screaming, and if I can't stop it then that's very difficult. If it's a pain then I may not be able to stop it. If he screams then that's *really* tiring – for me and the whole family.'

'I'm often completely exhausted – every weekend – because it's a long stretch of time with no help. We have no help over the weekend. We have to hoist David for everything he does – that takes time. We have to dress him, change nappies, feed him. And this all takes time. So there is no flow to the day – there are constant interruptions. Because David can't do that much for himself you tend to try to over-compensate – partly because it's stressful when he's not happy. The thing that is most difficult is constantly pushing him to be the best he could be.'

'Sometimes I am at my limit – intermittently. What gets me through is that we are still together as a family and I have my mother. Many families with children with PMLD have split up – it's proved too much for them. It's the "forever" factor – it's never going to go away. It's a lifelong job. To cope with this I break it down – one step or day at a time – I try not to think too far ahead.'

Other people don't understand

'Other people just don't understand. You know, you might go into the playground in a mainstream school and someone is stressing out that their child hasn't sorted out their phonemes. I would think: "How *lucky* are you that your child can walk and talk and play football!" You have a heightened awareness of what people take for granted. My friend would say: "I wish they were my worries."'

4 Concluding remarks

It would require a gifted writer to present a portrait of carers that succeeds in conveying the full range of their experience. The whole picture is likely to include a complicated 'inner' life, sometimes uninhibitedly talked about and shared with others, at other times concealed, shrugged off or denied. Nor are the complications confined to what goes on inside hearts and minds; carers' lives are complicated in ways that anyone can see, being called upon to protect, attend to and advocate on behalf of the people they care for, whilst coordinating the support and services without which their lives would become unsustainable.

And many aspects of carers' lives are not at all complex; on the contrary, they are uncomplicated and welcome – as with the pleasure derived from seeing a loved one taking her first unassisted steps, or simply, seeing her smile.

Fundamental is the fact of giving up much of one's own life to look after someone else. Some of those who care for a profoundly disabled person are making a large sacrifice; it is humbling to be in the presence of such people, their example calls for some acknowledgement, and that is one reason for writing this book.

Points for discussion

- 'Love – given and received – is the most precious aspect of care': discuss.
- Are some people more naturally equipped to care than others?
- 'The most difficult aspect of caring for a profoundly disabled child is the 'forever' factor': is it?
- Can anyone who is not a carer know what it's like to care for a profoundly disabled person?
- 'Good care depends as much on how society is organised as it does on individual carers'; do you agree?

9

CARING FOR PROFOUNDLY DISABLED PEOPLE

Reflection and theory

1 Introduction

Chapter 8 presented testimony from a handful of parents, and one grandparent. I could just as easily have included an account of the lives of any other carer who makes an appearance in this book. Their experiences would be different, but not altogether different: there are features of the lives depicted in these pages that many carers would recognise, and a few are worth returning to.

This last chapter offers a series of reflections on care and caring. I explore the process of adapting to life as a parent of a profoundly disabled child, some of the many dimensions of care and caring relations, and the place of reciprocity in relations between carer and cared-for. I end with some thoughts about what is hardest and also most precious about caring for profoundly disabled people.

2 Adapting to life as a carer

Naturally there are widely varying experiences of caring, and the differences may be stark, as illustrated here in how two mothers choose to describe their adaptation to an entirely new life. In *Welcome to Holland*, Emily Kingsley likened the arrival of a profoundly disabled new-born child to an unexpected holiday destination:

> When you're going to have a baby, it's like planning a fabulous vacation trip – to Italy. You buy a bunch of guide books and make your wonderful plans. The Coliseum. The Michelangelo David. The gondolas in Venice. You may learn some handy phrases in Italian. It's all very exciting.
>
> After months of eager anticipation, the day finally arrives. You pack your bags and off you go. Several hours later, the plane lands. The stewardess comes in and says, "Welcome to Holland." "Holland?!?" you say. "What do

you mean Holland?? I signed up for Italy! I'm supposed to be in Italy. All my life I've dreamed of going to Italy." But there's been a change in the flight plan. They've landed in Holland and there you must stay.

The important thing is that they haven't taken you to a horrible, disgusting, filthy place, full of pestilence, famine and disease. It's just a different place. So you must go out and buy new guide books. And you must learn a whole new language. And you will meet a whole new group of people you would never have met. It's just a different place. It's slower-paced than Italy, less flashy than Italy. But after you've been there for a while and you catch your breath, you look around ... and you begin to notice that Holland has windmills ... and Holland has tulips. Holland even has Rembrandts.

But everyone you know is busy coming and going from Italy ... and they're all bragging about what a wonderful time they had there. And for the rest of your life, you will say "Yes, that's where I was supposed to go. That's what I had planned." And the pain of that will never, ever, ever, ever go away ... because the loss of that dream is a very, very significant loss.

But ... if you spend your life mourning the fact that you didn't get to Italy, you may never be free to enjoy the very special, the very lovely things ... about Holland.

(1987: np)

This realistic but unambiguously positive analogy no doubt speaks for the experience of many parents, including many whose experience is presented elsewhere in this book. Parents recover from any shock and disappointment, adjust their expectations, and, in some cases, are able to say that they wouldn't have their lives, and, especially, their children, any other way.

Not all parents, however, could quite echo this last sentiment. We heard from Cheryl Arvidson-Keating in the Introduction. Her daughter, N, has multiple disabilities, including progressive cerebella ataxia, and it has taken Cheryl a long time to adjust to a life that includes looking after a profoundly dependent human being. During an especially difficult period, Cheryl wrote her own piece, *Welcome to Fucking Holland,* and this strikes a somewhat more sombre note than the original. Whilst the words to follow do not represent Cheryl's outlook generally, they provide a candid insight into how life can appear when someone is down on their knees. A few carers were prepared to disclose feelings of anger and resentment, but not many, and others were only willing to allude to – rather than discuss – these uncomfortable aspects of care. What follows surely captures something of what it is like for many people with highly dependent infants, tired beyond words and for whom there is no respite:

I am so bloody tired of everything. Five child-free days in Toulouse was wonderful ... Coming home and here I am again ... All I want to do is escape, either physically or in to my head ...

The house is full of specialist lifting equipment, wheelchairs, chairs, beds and bath-aids. N wants to hold her drink by herself and unless we supervise her constantly it spills. Everything is covered with juice – sofa, floor, chairs. The carpets need cleaning ... There is paperwork coming out the wazoo. If N doesn't have her splints and her shoes on all the time, she slips and falls, even with the walker. ...

B and I are living our lives, our marriage, in the cracks between caring for our child. Everything revolves around her. Our entire life is about her and her next move, whether that's forward or backwards. And today, I fucking resent it. I resent coming back from my five days just being me, just being Ally, who's in love with B.

I resent that I have a future that involves changing adult nappies and using a bath-lift and knackering my back lifting someone who doesn't have muscle control. I resent that we have to spend an hour and a half every day tube-feeding. I resent the time I spend on stretching exercises. I hate not getting proper sleep at night because when she wakes I lie there, rigid, waiting to see whether one of us is going to have to get out to turn her.

I resent the fact that I resent it all. I resent the fact that I am angry all the time ... I resent the time I spend filling in forms, talking to physiotherapists, talking to social workers. I resent not knowing where we are going in the future.

I resent the fact that my beautiful, clever, funny, amazing daughter, who I love so much it hurts, is not going to have the life that she should have had; and that we will not have that life we should have had with her.

I resent the fact that our entire fucking life has been hijacked by one measly gene fragment that doesn't even have the decency to be easily found.

Welcome to fucking Holland. It's shit here.

(Arvidson-Keating 2013: np)

This was written some time ago, during a period of depression – in Cheryl's case, 'reactive depression', a response to being overwhelmed – a diagnosis passed on both Cheryl and her husband. With the benefit of distance and hindsight, Cheryl can put these raw words in perspective; but she wouldn't, I think, erase them:

Looking back at 'Welcome to fucking Holland' now, I can see that I was in a very dark place when I wrote it – I was at rock bottom. And since then, we have had a lot more support put in place, we have a routine visit to the hospice every eight weeks, we have respite care about to kick in fortnightly, school transport has finally got itself sorted out and N's new school is working out brilliantly. I still feel like that occasionally; but I am in a much better place about it now. Retrospectively, I feel that it was a position I had to go through in order to come to terms with what is happening to us all.

(Ibid.)

Cheryl's testimony, including her retrospection, leads to an obvious question: how do people manage as parent-carers when sleeplessness is par for the course, when they must come to terms with the fact that they will never have anything like the life that they would have wanted for their children, and when a life of full-time caring stretches into the future with no end in sight? It should be said, first, that not everyone *is* able to cope: families break up, adults fall prey to clinical depression, and some parents find themselves having to place their children in the hands of others. But many do cope, if only because they have to: their children are utterly dependent upon them. And whilst one day may seem impossibly demanding, the next may be unpredictably easier. Parents adapt their expectations and their lives, and they tend (more or less) to adjust to living in Holland.

Adaptability is a significant phenomenon in the context of assessing the quality of people's lives. An outsider may only witness the initial grief of parents on first hearing a diagnosis that reveals profound disability, or their distress at watching their child endure acute respiratory complications that merit intensive care. Some time later, and the child and parents may have largely come to terms with their lives, and show themselves to be incomparably happier than anyone could have predicted whilst watching on in the intensive care unit.

The emotional profile of a carer is often complex, and not only because one day may be quite unlike another. A fair few of Cheryl's words could be uttered by many carers at the end of their tether, and it would take a person of unusual stoicism not to have some experience of despair in the midst of a long period of sleeplessness and unceasing demands. The chronicling of carers' lives should allow room for the whole gamut of emotions. And any account of caring that purports to be truthful, and neither partial nor delusively sanguine, must include an attempt to identify the complicated, ambivalent responses that carers do not find it easy to talk about.

3 Dimensions of caring

The complications extend not only to the emotional profiles of carers; they also include the many dimensions of caring that have been illustrated in recent testimony, and some of which I discuss here.

Know-how, advocacy, hard work

We have seen how much more there is to caring for others than showing them affection. Carers need knowledge of the medicines required, how and when to administer them, and how to clean and maintain any tubing and other apparatus; their schedule includes not only managing the routines of the cared-for, but also coordinating hospital visits and the support provided by such teams as the NHS Continuing Care Team. And if some service is not provided as it should be, the carer will often be called upon to act as an advocate. Advocacy demands assertiveness, a measure of belligerence, even. An advocate needs to know who it is best to talk to, or make demands of, and how most effectively to put the case in terms that are most likely to have the desired effect. So carers may have to learn how to 'operate' in public and political forums, and develop a preparedness to stick their neck out and become involved in protracted discussions and negotiations.

More than this, caring is often and simply hard work: it is taxing physically – the lifting and hoisting – and it is taxing emotionally – having to live with the needs, struggles and pains of the cared for. And it is often as taxing as it is because someone is responding to a need after a short or broken night's sleep. Sleep deprivation and chronic tiredness represent a significant threat to the capacity of carers to function effectively. It makes everything they do, starting with getting out of bed, inordinately harder than it would be if they were well rested. And it is not made any easier by the thought that the demands appear as never-ending; it is the 'forever-ness', the fact that carers often can't see any end in sight, that can make it difficult to muster enthusiasm for the day ahead. A catalogue of the labour involved in care, therefore, should document not only the tasks, activities and routines, along with the frequency and intensity of these, but also the support and resources available to the carer – immediate and extended family, professional care teams, labour-saving apparatus – including as these allow for rest and respite.

These preliminary reflections illustrate some of the many dimensions of caring, and their relative importance has been discussed by writers concerned with the ethics of care. In keeping with an emphasis on care as work, Fisher and Tronto focus on the physical labour involved: 'taking care of' is defined as 'everything that we do to maintain, continue and repair our "world" so that we can live in it as well as possible' (1990: 40). Noddings, however, emphasises the feelings, needs and desires of people who are cared for, and the ability sensitively and sympathetically to understand a situation from their point of view (2003: 14–19). Held concurs: those in caring relations should have a substantial capacity for being sensitive to the feelings of others (2006: 31–36).

Perhaps we should say that caring for profoundly disabled people involves *both* feelings and work, and this is consistent with the view that Noddings later arrives at:

> Care ... is *work* as well as an emotion or motive or intention ... Care is not *only* work, however. So it is not enough that the work get done and the child get fed if done without an appropriately caring motive. But, in my view, having caring motives is not enough to make one a caring person.'
>
> *(2003: 51).*

Sevenhuijsen takes a similar view: the caring person should be both attentive and responsive, and have the 'ability and a willingness to "see" and "hear" needs, and to take responsibility for these needs being met' (1998: 1, 83).

A significant question is whether any one or more of these elements is *necessary* to (good) caring, such that, in their absence, someone might be regarded as either not caring or not caring as they should. Is an element of physical labour, perhaps, necessary in this sense? Equally, we might ask which, if any, of these elements is *sufficient* for (good) caring, such that, so long as they are in evidence, someone may be thought of as a (good) carer even whilst not displaying some or all of the other caring-related attributes discussed here. Could either hard work or goodwill ever suffice? I return to these questions shortly.

Trust

Trust, perhaps, is the *sine qua non* of good care. For Held trust and care go hand in hand:

> To develop well and flourish, children need to trust those who care for them, and the providers of such care need to trust the fellow members of their communities that the trust of their children will not be misplaced. ... Care is not the same thing as trust, but caring relations should be characterised by trust, and caring and trust sustain each other.
>
> *(2006: 43)*

Trusting another person may be instinctual, or learned; it is also fragile and can be shattered by a single disappointment. Trust is a characteristic not only of individuals, and relations between individuals, but also of groups, institutions and societies. It is both a personal and a social asset and without it neither relationships nor societies can hope to thrive (ibid.: 56). Profoundly disabled people need to be able to trust their parents and carers but they also need to live in environments – homes, schools, residential accommodation – that are themselves characterised by high levels of trust and trustworthiness. Trust in all these senses was a distinguishing feature of each of the special schools that feature in this book, including as between learners and teachers, between teachers, and between teachers and parents.

I distinguished just now between trust and trustworthiness. Trust is an attitude that we have towards people whom we hope will be trustworthy; trustworthiness, however, is a property, not an attitude. Ideally, the people we trust are trustworthy, and people who are trustworthy will be trusted (McLeod 2014). Trusting someone generally requires that we can be vulnerable to them, think well of them, and remain optimistic that they are competent in how they treat us (ibid.). Profoundly disabled people are certainly vulnerable, and often think well of others, whilst also having confidence in their competence as carers. But not all profoundly disabled people 'think well' of their carers; some, perhaps are not capable of this thought, and some, certainly, are not capable of assessing the competence of people who look after them. Is, then, a cared-for person not capable of trusting others if she lacks the capacity to assess their competence, even whilst she shows pleasure and willing cooperation in their company? This seems unlikely, but to confirm this impression we would have to explore the relationship between the capacity to trust, on the part of profoundly disabled people, and their capacity to conceive of and expect competence on the part of their carers.

There is a further question, about whether the person who trusts – the trustor – should expect that the person she trusts – the trustee – will act from a certain kind of motive, and whether that motive is related to goodwill and care. Certainly people cannot trust one another if they are easily suspicious of each other; if a profoundly disabled person generally assumes the worst of her carers – that they will treat her meanly or take no account of her feelings – then this would more likely be a case of *distrusting* other people rather than trusting them (Govier 1997: 6). Trust, perhaps, involves being optimistic rather than pessimistic that trustees will do something positive for us (McLeod 2014). But is it also true that trust involves goodwill and a caring attitude? In the view of Baier it does (1986); she maintains that the trustworthy person should *care* about the trustor, and that caring and goodwill are central to trustworthiness. One reason for thinking that they are central is that it allows for a distinction between *trust* and *reliance*. Trust can be *betrayed*, whilst reliance can only be *disappointed*, for unlike reliance betrayal is a response to someone on whom one relied to act out of goodwill (Baier 1986: 234–235).

It would be better if carers acted out of goodwill, but is this *necessary* in order for the cared-for to trust them? Some profoundly disabled people will know very little about their carer, who on occasions will be new and unfamiliar. Can they not trust a new carer, knowing little about their motives, particularly if the carer proves herself to be competent, and even if competence does not always go hand in hand with goodwill? We cannot pursue this question, which is one of several raised here which go to the heart of the relationship between trust and caring.

Principles

Do carers (always) act on moral principles? Noddings suggests that they do not:

> [E]mpirical evidence suggests that individuals only rarely consult moral principles when making decisions that result in the prevention of harm. More often, people respond directly as carers (out of sympathy) or as faithful members of a community that espouses helping and not harming.
>
> *(2003: xv)*

This suggests that we should distinguish between caring behaviour that is explicitly understood by the carer as a response to a moral principle, and behaviour that is consistent with or conforms to that principle. I may not think about why I am feeding my infant son this morning, but my actions may nevertheless be consistent with the principle that I should help my dependents to feed themselves if they are unable to (ibid.). Moreover, whilst I may not *say* to myself that I should act so as to help my dependents, I may yet be motivated by a principle such as this, though it is now so thoroughly assimilated that I wouldn't even think to put it into words.

Kant famously said that we should 'act only according to that maxim whereby you can, at the same time, will that it should become a universal law' (2012: 37). In effect Kant is implying that I cannot consistently think that it is acceptable for me to lie in bed whilst my son goes hungry, if, were I in his place, and dependent on others for nourishment, I would expect to be looked after. If I think that some act is the right act for me, in my circumstances, then I must consistently think it would be the right act for anyone else in the same circumstances. In other words, the principle that 'I should get out of bed and feed my son' is 'universalisable' – it applies to anyone who is in the same position as I am. On Kant's view an act is morally right if and only if the underlying principle can consistently and universally apply to everyone.

Noddings does not accept this universalisability requirement:

> I … reject the notion of universalizability … I … want to preserve the uniqueness of human encounters. Since so much depends on the subjective experience of those involved in ethical encounters, conditions are rarely 'sufficiently similar' for me to declare that you must do what I must do.
>
> *(Ibid.: 5)*

Are all cases in which we are caring for someone else unique? Or, if not unique, then so distinctive that we should never say that, since I ought to do something on behalf of another, then so should you, if you were in my position? Even Noddings is reluctant to go so far; she finds that caring, and the commitment to sustain it, form the 'universal heart' of her ethical outlook:

> There is, however, a fundamental universality in our ethic … The caring attitude, that attitude which expresses our earliest memories of being cared for and our growing store of memories of both caring and being cared for, is universally accessible.
>
> *(Ibid.: 5–6)*

No one blueprint

Trust, principles, feelings, sensitivity, understanding, practical know-how, technical knowledge, advocacy and hard work: these are just some of the elements included in caring and caring relations. Not everyone will excel in all of these; nor – to suggest answers to some of the questions raised previously – should we therefore regard someone as failing to meet the standards associated with good care. There are people who are superb carers in virtue of hard work, conscientiousness, knowledgeableness and a basic kindness, though they may not always be especially warm and expressive. And there are people who are wonderful carers just in virtue of unerring instinct and insightful empathy that makes for an endless supply of 'human warmth', though they may not be well organised and would never profess to have the knowledge required to manage a complicated life-limiting condition. Any account of care should acknowledge both its multiple dimensions and the numerous ways in which it is possible to thrive (and fail) as a carer.

4 Dependency and reciprocity

There is one further aspect of caring for profoundly disabled people that calls for discussion, and that is the place of reciprocity in caring relations with people whose lives are characterised by dependency and vulnerability. Reciprocity has been discussed before, in Chapter 4 and elsewhere, but a few final comments are in order here.

Kittay defines dependency work as 'the work of caring for those who are inevitably dependent' (1999: ix), and the dependency relation is:

> a moral one arising out of a claim of vulnerability on the part of the dependent, on the one hand, and of the special positioning of the dependency worker to meet the need, on the other.
>
> *(Ibid.: 35)*

Noddings allows that the cared-for cannot always perform the same range of tasks as the carer, but whilst the carer can do more in this sense than the cared for, what they give to each other may balance out:

> by recognizing the carer's efforts, by responding in some positive way, the cared-for makes a distinctive contribution to the relation and establishes it as caring. In this way, infants contribute to the parent-child relation, patients to the physician-patient relation, and students to the teacher-student relation.
>
> *(2003: xiii–xiv)*

Noddings also draws attention to how much profoundly dependent people can give their carers, and those who come into contact with them, simply in virtue of being a nice or gentle person, or being always ready with a smile. It might be 'the infant's wriggles and smiles' or 'the patient's sigh of relief'; these, too, contribute to a caring relationship and to the efforts of the carer, for 'the contributions of the cared-for sustain us in our attempts to care' (ibid.: xiii–xiv).

At the same time it is essential to Noddings's account of caring that there is *some* element of reciprocity:

> The perception by the cared-for of an attitude of caring on the part of the one-caring is partially constitutive of caring … Caring involves two parties: the one caring and the cared-for. It is complete when it is fulfilled in both.
>
> *(Ibid.: 68)*

She acknowledges that some people cannot reciprocate in kind the care that they receive from others, but in that case what is important is that they should reciprocate in *some* way, if only in the form of showing some appreciative awareness of the caring received (ibid.: 86). Carers will almost always insist that there is some possibility of their care being reciprocated; it might not take the form of making an equal contribution to an activity shared between two people, but that takes nothing away from how much a carer values and appreciates a sign of gratitude, or relief, or pleasure: it might be a smile, a glance, even the twitch of an eyebrow.

Yet as we have seen, the capacity to reciprocate care can become significantly curtailed, and in some cases a person is able to respond to the efforts of carers only in the sense that their bodies are responding to interventions aimed at meeting their most basic needs. Is such a person capable of making any meaningful contribution to a caring relationship? Some carers of profoundly disabled children retort that it is precisely because the child in their care is so helpless and dependent that they are motivated and morally required to give them special attention. And they insist that even the slightest sign – a weak smile, a moment of stilled attention – is all that is required to motivate and reward their efforts. The extent of reciprocity is judged not only by the number and range of activities offered in response to a carer but also by what the acts and expressions of the cared-for signify and represent. Discussion of reciprocity in the context of profound disability should be sensitive to the apparently innocuous or unremarkable expressions which may yet mean a great deal to those who love them and know them best.

What of those people whose capacity for reciprocity is so slight that not even a smile is to be expected, as with Sam and Nadifa? A comprehensive account of caring should, perhaps, accommodate cases like these, explaining how people who are unable to reciprocate are, nevertheless, some part of a caring relation, not in virtue of what they do and express, but in virtue of who they are – or perhaps, as in cases of older people whose powers are comprehensively failing, who they once were.

5 The best and the worst

It is fitting to close with a few thoughts on what is hardest and most precious about caring for people with profound disabilities.

The hardest part

Many of the most difficult aspects of caring for dependent children are unsurprising: the children's physical pains and emotional frustrations, the parents' exhaustion and isolation. Some of what is most difficult stems from the prejudices of others, prejudices directed towards disability, race, and anyone who is 'other'; there are examples in this book of parents being excluded, shunned and attacked, whilst their children are mocked, derided and gawped at.

Parents also speak of how hard it is to accept a lack of control, particularly those formerly used to taking charge of their destiny. Your life is no longer yours in the way it was previously, since so much of what you now do is governed by what your child needs. You may have to give up your job, and the income and status that goes with that. You may not know what tomorrow will bring, including whether the arrangements you had put in place will work out as you had intended. Worse: the fate of your child is often not in your hands. For Heather the most difficult thing to deal with was seeing her grandchildren in distress and having no power to stop it: 'I want to help them, to take away their pain and discomfort, and I just can't – that's the most difficult thing.'

Parents may find themselves beset by the question, could I have done more for my child? The answer is likely to be 'No; you did all that anyone could have expected, more even', but that is not an answer all parents find it easy to accept. This is Jamila's pre-occupation: 'I love my children equally. But I wanted Omari to achieve and get somewhere. I haven't helped Ade out so much; I could have done more for him. He could have had speech. That's the thing I feel saddened about. When I speak to the teachers, they say "You've done your best." But I think that I should have done more for Ade.' No one with any understanding of what Jamila has lived with will be minded to agree with her self-assessment.

What is most precious?

What is most precious? The answer is almost always the same: love.

Jo, on her son Alex: 'He absolutely loves me, just as I absolutely love him.'

Sally, on her son Paul: 'The most precious thing is him. His love. ... It's all for him. All for him.'

Even at her lowest ebb, N is Cheryl's 'beautiful, clever, funny, amazing daughter, who I love so much it hurts.'

And for Heather, life, though tough, is rich: 'I would hate anyone to think that it's all doom and gloom. It's not. We have a very lively, happy, busy household with lots of visitors and love and fun to help us through the difficult stuff. And carers who are amazing and part of our family.' And there are wonderful moments too: 'Occasionally, when all the stars align, and all is right with the world, you get a glimmer of pure joy. It might be a response that makes you know you've broken through the wall, the barriers – I live for those moments! These might seem like small things, parents of well children may even take them for granted, but they're the things that we celebrate.'

6 Concluding remarks

The purpose of the discussion in this and the previous chapter has been to explore some of the many aspects of care: care as sheer hard, dutiful work and care as love and affection; from the most immediate and instinctive caring behaviour to the expert management of complex disorders and life-limiting conditions.

We have also looked at the place of reciprocity in good caring relations, acknowledging both the variable capacity to reciprocate and the many forms that reciprocity might take. The testimony presented throughout this book brings home the point that there are innumerable ways, some slight, subtle, and easily overlooked, in which profoundly disabled people can reciprocate the efforts of those who care for them.

The very best care is often the product of the efforts of a large number of people, and the contributions of carers themselves will likely prove as various as offering loving and patient company, feeding and toileting, lifting and hoisting, coordinating support and acting as an advocate. Caring is not a simple thing.

Points for discussion

- Does all good care require feelings of affection and warmth?
- To what extent is good care a product of skill and knowledge?
- 'Care is work'; is it?
- Is the capacity to reciprocate essential to a caring relationship?
- How can someone who cannot speak or vocalise, and who does not recognise her carers or what they do for her, contribute to a caring relationship?

10
LOOKING AHEAD

This book is designed to give voice to profound disability and I hope it has at least partially succeeded in doing that. Readers should have some insight into the lives and personalities of a small number of profoundly disabled people, and some idea of what it is like to care for and to live and work with them. For readers who already knew plenty, the portraits included here will, I trust, prove instantly recognisable, and, if not, then unfamiliar in ways that invite reflection on their own experience. It was also my intention that any discussion offered here, whether philosophical or otherwise, should serve to prompt reflection not only on any one child or carer or school, but also on some of the moral, social and political questions that arise when thinking about profound disability. And these broader questions, it turns out, have implications for everyone, in so far as we are or will become variously impaired, vulnerable and dependent.

The principal themes to emerge from the material gathered here are summarised at the end of each chapter. I won't repeat them all here. Rather, since this book represents only a small fraction of what might be written about profound disability, I will end by returning to subjects that I only touched on and which lend themselves to further exploration.

I should start by mentioning some of the numerous subjects barely commented on – personhood, for example, or identity, power, oppression and justice – and on which philosophers of disability have written extensively (Kittay 1999; Silvers 2000; Carlson 2010). There is a great deal more to say about these subjects as they apply to people who might be thought to lie at the 'margins of personhood' (Kittay 1999); or who are unable to withstand or campaign against a variety of oppressive practices – institutional, political and linguistic (Carlson 2010); or who cannot occupy an orthodox role in any theory of justice that assumes a contract of some sort between subjects who are parties to reciprocal moral and political relationships (Beaudry 2013).

These are questions that largely belong to the domain of social and political thought; others take us in the direction of moral philosophy. In discussing the value and moral status of profoundly disabled people, there are philosophers who concentrate almost exclusively on the psychological capacities of human beings; some also comparing these – not always favourably – with the capacities of other animals (McMahan 2002; Singer 1979). To many readers it will seem offensive, or just plain wrong-headed, to compare the value of any human being with any non-human animal, at least if any such comparison is thought not to favour the human being. But whatever we want to say about the outcome of any such exercise, the exercise itself is not one to be avoided. We should face the question, for example, why we value Nadifa or Sam more than any other non-human animal, particularly if we acknowledge that some non-human animals have a greater range of capabilities and psychological capacities. To ask this question is *not* to assume that we might value Nadifa and Sam less than some other non-human animals. It is, rather, simply to encourage reflection on the value we attribute to human beings and the reasons why we do so.

Some philosophers – Mulhall and Diamond, for example – maintain that there is something fundamentally misguided about comparing the value of human and non-human animals by means of conducting an audit of their capabilities. We are to look not only or primarily at human beings as a neurologist or cognitive psychologist might, but rather to see them imaginatively – as having a human fate, as being our fellow creatures who share in our common life. In thinking about the worth of human beings we should exercise what Rowan Williams has called 'imaginative charity'; and we should take seriously the meaning of a human life and the culture that human beings live under, which is quite different from anything that applies to the non-human animal kingdom. Thoughts of this kind express something true and important, but McMahan's forensic criticism is telling; there is much more to be written about the role of imagination and the place of meaningfulness in conceiving human value so as to avoid the obscurities that characterise some of the existing attempts.

It is one thing to ask about someone's value, another to ask about their moral status. For Kant, as we saw, all rational, autonomous beings are 'ends in themselves', and it is the capacity for autonomy and rationality that accounts for a dignity and value that is elevated above any price. The implications of Kant's work for people with disabilities have long been discussed by philosophers (Nussbaum 2008; Cureton 2007), including whether his arguments would have the effect of excluding some disabled people from the 'Kingdom of Ends'. Kant writes: '*Autonomy* is thus the ground of the dignity of a human and of every rational creature' (2102: 48). But do all people with profound disabilities have the autonomy that Kant demands? And what are we to conclude if they do not? Freedom, autonomy and independence are among the values that lie at the centre of pervasive moral and political belief systems. But there remain fundamental questions as to whether human beings *are* indeed as free, or autonomous or independent as the orthodoxy would have it. Like many feminist and other writers, I suggest that all human beings, and not only those with extensive disabilities, are variously dependent and interdependent on a scale that implies that we have exaggerated and misconceived the scope for human autonomy and independence. Our dependence, interdependence and interconnectedness prompt significant questions about our nature and status – as individuals, as members of groups, and in the context of our relations to each other (Kittay 1999). Even supposing it is an exaggeration to claim that these questions apply to all human beings, they undoubtedly apply to the very sizeable number of people whose dependencies are extensive simply in virtue of being very young, old, frail, ill, diseased, disabled, poor or unemployed.

I elected not explicitly to discuss questions about the quality of people's lives, and how this is best thought about and assessed. This subject increasingly attracts the attention of philosophers and medical ethicists, including the impact of disability on the quality of life, and, in the most extreme cases, the implications for decisions about whether it is the right thing to preserve a life (Wilkinson 2013). These are among the hardest questions that confront parents and clinicians, as when they are faced with a decision about what to do for a child with a life-limiting condition, reaching the end of his life in a lot of pain, his organs failing and whose complications are daily getting worse. Nor is it always possible to ignore the claim on resources required to keep a child alive; the teams responsible for making any such decision will know that, if they choose to preserve one life, and to provide the necessary medications and facilities to do that, they may not always also be able to provide the same resources to sustain another life, equally precious and equally loved by their nearest and dearest. There are often almost impossibly hard choices to be made, and in order to assist understanding of what is at stake, it will be necessary both to learn from the personal and professional experience of those directly involved and to engage those whose expertise ranges from neurology to moral philosophy.

Turning now to the testimony gathered in this book: this represents only a small sample of what might have been included, and in the main interviewees are either carers or teachers. The emphasis might have been different: less on family and education and more on nursing, clinical and therapeutic contexts; or less on human testimony from whatever source and more on neurological and other scientific evidence. Nevertheless, there is a great deal more to be done in the way of documenting the experiences of carers and teachers. It would be valuable, for example, to compile evidence from ethnographic studies of families, or schools, or residential homes, observing the lives of children and adults with profound disabilities over several years, and the lives of those who live with and care for them.[1] Or, to contemplate an exercise of a different kind, it should be possible to undertake an international and comparative study, looking into the similarities and differences in the experience of profound disability as between two or more countries within the European Union, or between European and non-European countries. There are numerous possibilities for social scientists in the way of providing both insightful portraits of individual people and settings, and gathering data on large numbers of profoundly disabled people, their carers and teachers, in numerous regions around the world.

Not that these exercises should engage only social scientists. The potential for collaboration is obvious: between practitioners – teachers, carers, musicians, actors, therapists, nurses or neuro-disability specialists; or between practitioners and the academic community – philosophers, sociologists, psychologists, educationalists, epidemiologists and neuroscientists. My assumption is that, in the main, anyone writing about disability should feel bound to work with empirical evidence – whether drawn, as here, from human testimony – or from recent advances in such fields as neuro-science, communicative technology and speech and language therapy.

A few more illustrations of the scope for collaborative enquiry: one subject of this book, and one subject of great interest to philosophers, is human capabilities, including as these allow a person to relate and respond to others and to communicate on their own behalf. Teachers and therapists, using the best available technology, therapy and pedagogy, are often able to develop a communicative repertoire that might have seemed unreachable to the uninitiated. Philosophers can learn not only about what is possible communicatively, but also how progress in communication is encouraged, achieved and valued; how what might appear as insignificant to an observer – someone using two keys on a keypad rather than one – is to the typist, and their teacher, an achievement that means everything in the world. '*Small steps!*' is a message repeatedly heard in these pages: whether a person can now type two words rather than one; take six unassisted steps rather than four; or brush their teeth for ten seconds rather than five. To understand progress of this kind, its significance for those who achieve it, and for those who encouraged it, it is, to say the least, helpful for academics to spend time with those involved, when they might also be exposed to such non-verbal forms of communication as Emma's 'being with' communication – communication between one person and another that takes place without words, but which includes some understanding and pleasure derived just by being close to and spending time with a loved one.

Communicative possibilities are significant in the political domain too. A profoundly disabled person may never participate in politics in ways that are open to most of us. But if she is able to indicate even a basic set of preferences to someone with the knowledge and authority to use these as evidence of what is in her best interests, then this opens up possibilities for how a guardian or a trustee might act on her behalf, whether in the context of her family and school, or in the wider arena of local and national political decision-making (Nussbaum 2006). Here there is scope for collaboration between speech and language therapists, interpreters and advocates, and academics who work on theories of justice and political philosophy.

One subject not dwelt upon in this book, but endlessly discussed, not only by philosophers, but also by religious writers, psychologists, and novelists, is the question of what it is to be a human being, or a person. Of course, developments in the sciences, and in neuro-science especially, will extend our knowledge of the mechanisms that explain the nature and development of human capability and potential. But it is not the sciences alone from which more understanding of personhood is to be gained. To take just two examples, performing artists and musicians can help us to think about these questions, by encouraging and enabling profoundly disabled people to do something quintessentially human – laughing, for example, or playing music. These activities can reveal a level of understanding and sensitivity that might not have been anticipated, as when, for example, a child notices something incongruous about an adult clown whose trousers are falling down, and roars with laughter; or when an adult who is unable to use language is found to be able to play and respond to the music of J.S. Bach. What can we learn about being human from people who cannot do what most human beings can do, but who can also share a laugh with us or immerse themselves in music? The study of laughter or music making in the company of artists and performers can provide insight into human capabilities and potentialities that we might otherwise easily miss.

These are just a few of the numerous possibilities for research that lie ahead. And there is one last: it should be, as in fact it is, a priority to utilise the latest pedagogic, therapeutic and technological developments, above all so as to enable people with profound disabilities to communicate with others and to engage with the world, but also to enable them to participate in any attempt to document their lives and experience. It is certainly not inconceivable that a study on the subjects presented here should one day include the voices of the people this book is most centrally about.

Note

1   An ethnographic study is based on extensive fieldwork, over a sustained period, and the researcher either lives with or is otherwise immersed in the lives of the people being observed. A study of profoundly disabled people of just this kind is underway in Finland, led by Simo Vehmas.

FURTHER PHILOSOPHICAL READING

I could fill many pages with details of books and articles that I have learned from. Instead, I will mention just a tiny fraction of the philosophical material that I found most valuable, for readers who are new to this subject, and who would like to know more.

Starting with writers who in their different ways are taken up with questions about *equality, difference and oppression*. Like many others I have a debt to Eva Kittay, for her work as a philosopher, and her shared experience as the mother of a profoundly disabled daughter. She offers both philosophical and personal reflection in Kittay 1999, *Love's Labor: Essays on Women, Equality and Dependency* (Routledge). Anita Silvers is a pioneering philosopher with personal experience of disability, and whose impressive range encompasses philosophy, law, feminism and bioethics. For an example, see Silvers et al. 1998, *Disability, Difference, Discrimination: Perspectives on Bioethics and Public Policy* (Rowman and Littlefield). Licia Carlson displays acute philosophical insight in her writing on disability and she has a keen understanding of its sociological dimensions – see Carlson 2010 *The Faces of Intellectual Disability: Philosophical Reflections* (Indiana University Press), and also her collaboration with Kittay, in Kittay and Carlson 2010, *Cognitive Disability and its Challenge to Moral Philosophy* (Wiley-Blackwell).

Martha Nussbaum is a world-renowned philosopher whose work on *human capabilities* is both inspiring and challenging – see Nussbaum 2006, *Frontiers of Justice* (Harvard University Press). Christopher Liddle examines how the experience of disability is accounted for in the capabilities approach to justice – Liddle 2014, *Disability & Justice: The Capabilities Approach in Practice* (Lexington Books). Lorella Terzi has written extensively on capability theory as this applies to disability and education – see Terzi 2010, *Justice and Equality in Education: A Capability Perspective on Disability and Special Educational Needs* (Continuum).

Raymond Gaita and Cora Diamond write with elegance and sensitivity on *the value and moral status of human beings* – see Gaita 2000, *A Common Humanity: Thinking*

134 Further philosophical

about Love and Truth and Justice (Routledge), and Diamond 1978, 'Eating Meat and Eating People', *Philosophy*, 53, 206: 465–479. Jeff McMahan reaches conclusions that many people who care for and work with profoundly disabled people will find distasteful and uncomfortable. However, his work is undeniably impressive and outstandingly lucid – see McMahan 2002, *The Ethics of Killing, Problems at the Margins of Life* (Oxford University Press). Hans Reinders discusses the moral implications of developments in genetics for people with disabilities, in Reinders 2000, *The Future of the Disabled in a Liberal Society: An Ethical Analysis* (Notre Dame Press). A significant new work is being prepared by Chrissie Rogers, who brings both philosophical and sociological perspectives to bear on the subject of being human – see Rogers (forthcoming), *Intellectual Disability and Social Theory: Philosophical Debates on Being Human* (Routledge). Simo Vehmas has written extensively on profound disability – see, for example, Curtis and Vehmas 2013, 'Moral Worth and Severe Intellectual Disability – A Hybrid View', in Bickenbach et al. (eds), *Disability and the Good Human Life* (Cambridge University Press). I should also draw attention to a groundbreaking project, closely related to many of the themes pursued in this book, and exploring the question 'What makes a good life for people with profound disabilities?' Vehmas and colleagues will gather evidence in Finland from adults with PMLD, their family members and caring staff. Details of progress are available at: www.aka.fi/en-GB/A/Academy-of-Finland/.

In almost all philosophical writing on *dignity and respect* the work of Immanuel Kant looms large. His most famous work on this subject – short, but very difficult – is Kant 1785, *Groundwork of the Metaphysics of Morals*. The Gregor and Timmermann 2012 edition (Cambridge University Press) includes a helpful introduction. Nussbaum discusses dignity in relation to human capabilities – see Nussbaum 2008, 'Human Dignity and Political Entitlements', in *Human Dignity and Bioethics*, Washington DC, 'The President's Council on Bioethics': 351–380. Adam Cureton explores Kantian themes as these apply to people with disabilities – see, for example, Cureton, 2007, 'Respecting Disability' in *Teaching Philosophy*, 30, 4: 383–402.

The voluminous literature on the *ethics of care* includes Kittay 1999, mentioned above. Nel Noddings published a seminal text in 1984, since published in a revised edition – see Noddings 2003, *Caring: A Feminine Approach to Ethics and Moral Education* (University of California Press). Virginia Held provides a penetrating review of philosophical accounts of care in Held 2006, *The Ethics of Care* (Oxford University Press). The work of Diemut Bubeck is well worth visiting – see Bubeck 1995, *Care, Gender, and Justice* (Oxford University Press), as is the work of Joan Tronto – see Fisher and Tronto 1990, 'Toward a Feminist Theory of Caring', in Abel and Nelson (eds) *Circle of Care* (SUNY Press).

REFERENCES

Only materials referred to in the text are included here.

American Psychiatric Association, 2000, *Diagnostic and Statistical Manual of Mental Disorders*, 4th edn (DSM-IV-TR), Arlington, VA: American Psychiatric Association.

American Psychiatric Association, 2013, *Diagnostic and Statistical Manual of Mental Disorders*, 5th edn, Arlington, VA: American Psychiatric Association.

Ansdell, G., 2014, *How Music Helps: A Perspective from Music Therapy*, Aldershot: Ashgate.

Arvidson-Keating, C., 2013, *Welcome to Fucking Holland*, posted on Writers Anon – Taunton's Writing Group, http://writersanontaunton.wordpress.com/2013/11/25/welcome-to-fking-holland-by-cheryl-arvidson-keating/.

Arvidson-Keating, C., 2014, *You can't take the sky away from me*, personal blog, 25 June, www.welcometoholland.co.uk/search?updated-min=2014–01–01T00:00:00Z&updated-max=2015–01–01T00:00:00Z&max-results=50.

Baier, A., 1986, 'Trust and antitrust', *Ethics*, 96: 231–260.

Beauchamp, T., and Childress, J., 1983, *Principles of Biomedical Ethics*, 2nd edn, New York: Oxford University Press.

Beaudry, J.-S., 2013, 'Can social contract theory fully account for the moral status of profoundly disabled people', unpublished DPhil thesis, University College, Oxford.

Boddington, P., and Podpadec, T., 1991, 'Who are the mentally handicapped?', *Journal of Applied Philosophy*, 8, 2: 177–190.

Boyle, M., forthcoming, 'Essentially rational animals', in Abel, G., and Conant, J. (eds), *Rethinking Epistemology*, Berlin, Germany: Walter de Grutyer, http://dash.harvard.edu/handle/1/8641838.

Brett, J., 2002, 'The experience of disability from the perspective of parents of children with profound impairment: is it time for an alternative model of disability?', *Disability & Society*, 17, 7: 825–843.

Burchardt, T., 2004, 'Capabilities and disability: the capabilities framework and the social model of disability', *Disability and Society* 19, 7: 735–751.

Carlson, L., 2010, *The Faces of Intellectual Disability*, Bloomington and Indianapolis: Indiana University Press.

Chappell, A.L., 2000, 'Emergence of participatory methodology in learning difficulty research: understanding the context', *British Journal of Learning Disabilities*, 28: 38–43.

Children and Families Act, 2014, London: Department for Education.

Cigman, R., 2013, 'Education without condescension: philosophy, personhood and cognitive disability', in Florian, L. (ed.), *SAGE Handbook of Special Education*, London: SAGE, chapter 47.

Cleland, C., 1979, *The Profoundly Mentally Retarded*, Englewood Cliffs, NJ: Prentice-Hall.

Cohen, G.A., 2011, *On the Currency of Egalitarian Justice, and Other Essays in Political Philosophy*, Princeton, NJ: Princeton University Press.

Colley, A., 2013, *Personalised Learning for Young People with Profound and Multiple Learning Difficulties*, London: Jessica Kingsley.

Corbett, J., 1992, 'Careful teaching: researching a special career', *British Educational Research Journal*, 18, 3: 235–243.

Corbett, J., and Norwich, B., 1999, 'Learners with special educational needs', in Mortimore, P. (ed.), *Understanding Pedagogy and its Impact on Learning*, London: Paul Chapman, 115–136.

Cureton, A., 2007, 'Respecting disability', *Teaching Philosophy* 30, 4: 383–402.

Dee, L., et al., 2002, *Enhancing Quality of Life: A Literature Review*, Cambridge: University of Cambridge.

Dennett, D., 1978, 'Conditions of personhood', in Dennett, D., *Brainstorms*, Brighton: Manchester Press, 267–285.

Department for Education, 2010, *Progression 2010–11: Advice on Improving Data to Raise Attainment and Maximise the Progress of Learners with Special Educational Needs*, London: Department for Education.

Department for Education, 2014, *Performance – P Scale – Attainment Targets for Pupils with Special Educational Needs*, London: Department for Education.

Diamond, C., 1991, 'The importance of being human', in Cockburn, D. (ed.), *Human Beings*, Cambridge: Cambridge University Press, 35–62.

Disability and Society, 1999, 'Special issue: theory and experience', *Disability and Society*, 14, 5.

Disability Discrimination Act (DDA) 1995 and 2005.

DiSilvestro, R., 2010, *Human Capacities and Moral Status*. Dordrecht: Springer.

Emerson, E., 2009, *Estimating Future Numbers of Adults with Profound Multiple Learning Difficulties in England*, Lancaster: Centre for Disability Research, Lancaster University.

Emerson, E., and Hatton, C., 2008, *Estimating Future Need for Adult Social Care Services for People with Learning Disabilities in England*, Lancaster: Centre for Disability Research, Lancaster University.

Fisher, B., and Tronto, J., 1990, 'Toward a feminist theory of caring', in Abel, E., and Nelson, M. (eds), *Circle of Care*, Albany, NY: SUNY Press, 36–54.

Fitton, P., 1994, *Listen to Me – Communicating the Needs of People with Profound Intellectual and Multiple Physical Disabilities*, London and Bristol: Jessica Kingsley.

Francis, L., and Silvers, A. (eds), 2000, *Americans with Disabilities: Exploring Implications of the Law for Individuals and Institutions*, London: Routledge.

Frankfurt, H., 1971, 'Freedom of the will and the concept of a person', *The Journal of Philosophy*, 68, 1: 5–20.

Frankfurt, H., 1999, 'Equality and respect', in Frankfurt, H., *Necessity, Volition and Love*, Cambridge: Cambridge University Press, 146–154.

Frankfurt, H., 2004, *The Reasons of Love*, Princeton and Oxford: Princeton University Press.

Fraser, N., and Gordon, L., 1977, 'Dependency' demystified: inscriptions of power in a keyword of the Welfare State, in Goodin, R., and Pettit, P. (eds), *Contemporary Political Philosophy*, Oxford: Blackwell, 618–633.

Gaita, R., 2000, 'Goodness beyond virtue', in *A Common Humanity*, 2nd edn, London: Routledge, 17–27.

Gaita, R., 2004, *Good and Evil, An Absolute Conception*, 2nd edn, London: Routledge.

Goffman, E., 1991, *Asylums*, Harmondsworth: Penguin Books.

Goode, D.,1984, 'Socially produced identities, intimacy and the problem of competence among the retarded', in Barton, L., and Tomlinson, S. (eds), *Special Education and Social Interests*, Beckenham: Croom Helm, 228–248.

Govier, T., 1997, *Social Trust and Human Communities*, Montreal and Kingston: McGill-Queen's University Press.

Held, V., 2006, *The Ethics of Care: Personal, Political and Global*, Oxford: Oxford University Press.

Hobbs, V., 2014, 'What do practitioners believe are the elements, conditions, factors and considerations that contribute to the provision of an appropriate and relevant learning environment for pupils with Profound and Multiple Learning Difficulties?', unpublished report for Associateship, Institute of Education.

Hogg, J., and Sebba, J., 1986, *Profound Retardation and Multiple Impairment: Volume 2, Education and Therapy*, London: Croom Helm.

Imray, P., and Hinchcliffe, V., 2013, *Curricula for Teaching Children and Young People with Severe or Profound and Multiple Learning Difficulties: Practical Strategies for Educational Professionals*, London: Routledge.

Kant, I., 2012, *Groundwork of the Metaphysics of Morals*, ed. Gregor, M., and Timmerman, J., Cambridge: Cambridge University Press.

Kingsley, E., 1987, *Welcome to Holland*, www.our-kids.org/Archives/Holland.html.

Kittay, E., 1999, *Love's Labor: Essays on Women, Equality and Dependency*, New York: Routledge.

Kittay, E., 2001, 'When caring is justice and justice is caring: justice and mental retardation', *Public Culture*, 13, 3: 557–579.

Kittay, E., 2005, 'At the margins of moral personhood', *Ethics* 116: 100–131.

Kittay, E., 2009, 'The ethics of philosophizing: ideal theory and the exclusion of people with severe cognitive disabilities', in Tessman, L. (ed.), *Feminist Ethics and Social and Political Philosophy: Theorizing the Non-Ideal*, Dordrechet: Springer, 121–146.

Kittay, E., 2010, 'The personal is philosophical is political: a philosopher and mother of a cognitively disabled person sends notes from the battlefield', in Kittay, E., and Carlson, L. (eds), *Cognitive Disability and its Challenge to Moral Philosophy*, Oxford: Wiley-Blackwell, 393–413.

Knox, M., Mok, M., and Parmenter, T., 2000, 'Working with the experts: collaborative research with people with an intellectual disability', *Disability and Society* 15, 1: 1–15.

Lacey, P., 1998, 'Meeting complex needs through multidisciplinary teamwork', in Lacey, P. and Ouvry C. (eds), *People with Profound and Multiple Learning Difficulties: A Collaborative Approach to Meeting Complex Needs*, London: David Fulton Publishers, ix–xvii.

Longhorn, F., 2010, *A Sensory Curriculum for Very Special People*, London: Souvenir Press Limited.

Macleod, C., 2010, 'Primary goods, capabilities and children', in Brighouse, H., and Robeyns, I. (eds), *Measuring Justice: Primary Goods and Capabilities*, Cambridge: Cambridge University Press, 174–192.

Male, D., 2009, 'Who goes to SLD schools? A follow up study', *Educational and Child Psychology*, 26, 4: 19–30.

Male, D., and Rayner, M., 2007, 'Who goes to SLD schools? Aspects of policy and provision for pupils with profound and multiple learning difficulties who attend special schools in England', *Support for Learning*, 22, 3: 145–152.

Margalit, A., 1996, *The Decent Society*, Cambridge, MA: Harvard University Press.

McLeod, Carolyn, 2014, 'Trust', *The Stanford Encyclopedia of Philosophy*, summer edn, Edward N. Zalta (ed.), http://plato.stanford.edu/archives/sum2014/entries/trust/.

McMahan, J., 2002, *The Ethics of Killing,* Oxford: Oxford University Press.

McMahan, J., 2005, 'Our Fellow Creatures', *The Journal of Ethics,* 9: 353–380.

Michael, J., and the Independent Inquiry into Access to Healthcare for People with Learning Disabilities, 2008, *Healthcare for All,* London: Department of Health.

Midgley, M., 1985, 'Persons and non-persons', in Singer, P. (ed.), *In Defence of Animals,* Oxford, Basil Blackwell, 52–62.

Mortimore, P. (ed.), 1999, *Understanding Pedagogy and its Impact on Learning,* London: Paul Chapman.

Mulhall, S., 2002, 'Fearful Thoughts', in *London Review of Books,* 24, 16: 16–18.

Ndaji, F., and Tymms, P., 2009, *The P scales: Assessing the Progress of Children with Special Educational Needs,* Oxford: Wiley Blackwell.

Noddings, N., 2003, *Caring: A Feminine Approach to Ethics and Moral Education,* 2nd edn, Berkeley: University of California Press.

Norris, D., 1982, *Profound Mental Handicap,* Tunbridge Wells: Ostello Educational.

Nozick, R., 1997, 'Do animals have rights?' in Nozick, R., *Socratic Puzzles,* Cambridge, MA: Harvard University Press, 305–310.

Nussbaum, M., 2006, *Frontiers of Justice. Disability, Nationality, Species Membership,* Cambridge, MA: Harvard University Press.

Nussbaum, M., 2008, 'Human dignity and political entitlements', in The *President's Council on Bioethics, Human Dignity* and *Bioethics,* Washington, DC, 351–380.

Nussbaum, M., 2009, 'The capabilities of people with cognitive disabilities', *Metaphilosophy,* 40, 3–4: 331–351.

Ockleford, A., 2008, *Music for Children and Young People with Complex Needs,* Oxford: Oxford University Press.

Ouvry, C., 1987, *Educating Children with Profound Handicaps,* Kidderminster: British Institute of Mental Handicap.

Rachels, J., 1986, *The End of Life: Euthanasia and Morality,* Oxford: Oxford University Press.

Raz, J., 2002, 'On Frankfurt's explanation of respect for people', in Bass, S., and Overton, L. (eds), *Contours of Agency: Essays in Honour of Harry Frankfurt,* Cambridge, MA: MIT Press.

Salt, T., 2010, *Salt Review: Independent Review of Teacher Supply for Pupils with Severe, Profound and Multiple Learning Difficulties (SLD and PMLD),* London: Department of Children School and Families.

Scanlon, T., 2000, *What We Owe To Each Other,* Cambridge, MA: Harvard University Press.

Sen, A., 1984, 'Rights and capabilities', in Sen, A., *Resources, Values and Development,* Oxford: Blackwell, 307–324.

Sen, A., 1985, *Commodities and Capabilities,* Amsterdam: North-Holland.

Sen, A., 1992, *Inequality Reexamined,* Oxford. Oxford University Press.

Sevenhuijsen, S., 1998, *Citizenship and the Ethics of Care: Feminist Considerations on Justice, Morality and Politics,* London, Routledge.

Silvers, A., 1995, 'Reconciling equality to difference: caring (f)or justice for people with disabilities', *Hypatia,* 10.1: 30–55.

Silvers, A., Wasserman, D., and Mahowald, M., 1998, *Disability, Difference, Discrimination: Perspectives on Justice in Bioethics and Public Policy,* Lanham, MD: Rowman and Littlefield.

Singer, P., 1979, *Practical Ethics,* Cambridge: Cambridge University Press.

Smith, S., 2001, 'Distorted ideals: the "problem of dependency" and the mythology of independent living', *Social Theory and Practice,* 27, 4: 579–598.

Special Educational Needs and Disability Act 2001.

Tassé, M., Luckasson, R., and Nygren, M., 2013, 'AAIDD proposed recommendations for ICD–11 and the condition previously known as mental retardation', *Intellectual and Developmental Disabilities,* 51, 2: 127–131.

Taylor, C., 1992, *Sources of the Self,* Cambridge, MA: Harvard University Press.

Terzi, L., 2007, 'Capability and educational equality: the just distribution of resources to students with disabilities and special educational needs', *Journal of Philosophy of Education*, 41, 4: 757–773.

Terzi, L., 2010, *Justice and Equality in Education: A Capability Perspective on Disability and Special Educational Needs*, London: Continuum.

Tetzchner, S., and Jensen, K., 1999, 'Interacting with people who have severe communication problems: ethical considerations', *International Journal of Disability, Development and Education*, 46, 4: 456–457.

The Americans with Disabilities Act Amendments Act, 2008.

United Nations General Assembly, 1948, *Universal Declaration of Human Rights*.

Watson, J., and Fisher, A., 1997, 'Evaluating the effectiveness of intensive interactive teaching with pupils with profound and complex learning difficulties', *British Journal of Special Education*, 24, 2: 80–87.

Weil, S., 2005, *Simone Weil: An Anthology*, ed. Miles, S., London: Penguin Books.

Wilkinson, D., 2013, *Death or Disability: The 'Carmentis Machine' and Decision-making for Critically Ill Children,* Oxford: Oxford University Press.

Williams, B., 1973, 'The idea of equality', in Williams, B., *Problems of the Self*, Cambridge: Cambridge University Press, 230–249.

Wittgenstein, L., 1998, *Culture and Value*, ed. von Wright, G.H., Oxford: Blackwell.

World Health Organisation, 1992, *The ICD-10 Classification of Mental and Behavioural Disorders: Clinical Descriptions and Diagnostic Guidelines*, Geneva: World Health Organisation.

INDEX